Stress Less, Pregnant Mom

This book belongs to:

_____

Please contact me if found:

_____

Stress Less, Pregnant Mom

From Clueless to Confident
with Guided Monthly Checklists,
Worksheets, and Must-Know Info

**Michelle Newman +
Brinya Van Guilder**

LONGBOAT PRESS

To you, pregnant mom-to-be.

Interior book design and illustrations by Karen Hood
Edited by Katie Elia

Library of Congress Control Number: 2024902194

Publisher's Cataloging-in-Publication Data

Names: Newman, Michelle, 1990- , author. | Van Gulder, Brinya, 1989- , author.
Title: Stress less, pregnant mom : from clueless to confident with guided monthly checklists, worksheets, and must-know info / Michelle Newman + Brinya Van Guilder.
Description: Sarasota, FL : Longboat Press, 2024. | Summary: This pregnancy guide has checklists, essential information, and worksheets for each trimester to help mothers stay informed and organized throughout pregnancy and to prepare for the transition to motherhood.
Identifiers: LCCN 2024902194 | ISBN 9798989953905 (paperback) | ISBN 9798989953912 (hardcover) | ISBN 9798989953929 (ebook)
Subjects: LCSH: Pregnant women – Health and hygiene – Popular works. | Pregnancy – Popular works. | Pregnancy – Psychological aspects – Popular works. | Childbirth – Popular works. | BISAC: HEALTH & FITNESS / Pregnancy & Childbirth. | FAMILY & RELATIONSHIPS / Parenting / Motherhood. | FAMILY & RELATIONSHIPS / Life Stages / Infants & Toddlers.
Classification: LCC RG525.N49 2024 | DDC 618.2 N--dc23
LC record available at https://lccn.loc.gov/2024902194

ISBN 979-8-9899539-0-5 (paperback)
ISBN 979-8-9899539-1-2 (hardcover)
ISBN 979-8-9899539-2-9 (ebook)

A Gift for You

To say thank you for reading our book, we would like to give you our **Baby Prep Toolkit** for free. We've found that the moms-to-be who download, read, and bring our toolkit to the hospital on labor day are among the most informed and organized new moms on the (hospital floor) block.

STRESSLESSMOM.COM/FREEDOWNLOADS

If, at any time, you feel that you need extra support to get organized while you're reading this book, you can schedule a **"V.I.Pregnancy" consultation** with our team. We will help put a game plan in place for knocking out your to-do's and finding the best path forward for your confident transition from pregnancy to motherhood.

STRESSLESSMOM.COM/VIPREGNANCY

Scan to Download Now

Contents

Introduction **10**

Countdown to Baby: The Week-by-Week Must-Do Checklist **12**

FIRST TRIMESTER (WEEKS 1-13)

I'm Pregnant, Now What? Early First Trimester Checklist **18**

First Trimester Checklist **20**

Food and Drinks to Avoid + Cooking Reminders **23**

Medical History + Questions
   to Ask at the First OB/GYN Appointment **26**

Medical History Worksheet **27**

Questions to Ask Your OB/GYN **34**

Medication List Worksheet **37**

Maternity Leave Request Emails + Other Templates **38**

My Prenatal Appointments **42**

First Ultrasound Photo **43**

SECOND TRIMESTER (WEEKS 14-27)

Second Trimester Checklist **46**

Baby Registry Checklist **48**

Monthly Budget for Baby **52**

Baby Registry 101 . . . . **53**

Sharing the Load with Your Partner Worksheet **58**

Ways Your Partner Can Help Postpartum **59**

Questions to Ask a Potential Doula **61**

Questions to Ask a Potential Daycare **66**

Questions to Ask a Potential Babysitter **72**

Favorite Baby Names Worksheet **74**

20 Week Ultrasound Photo **75**

THIRD TRIMESTER (WEEKS 28-40+)

Third Trimester Checklist **78**

Questions to Ask on a Hospital Tour **80**

Questions to Ask a Potential Pediatrician **90**

What to Pack in Your Hospital Bag **92**

Essential Documents for the Hospital on Labor Day **94**

Birth Preferences Worksheet **95**

Breastfeeding Essentials + Tips **96**

Breast Milk Storage + How to Thaw **98**

Formula Feeding Essentials + Tips **99**

Safe Sleep 101 . . . . **100**

Baby Caretaking Rules **102**

Our Caretaking Rules Worksheet **103**

Kick Counter Fetal Movement Log **104**

Baby Registry Gift Log **111**

FINAL PREPARATIONS

What to Stock Up On Before Baby Arrives. **116**

Ways to Care for Yourself as a New Mom **117**

Postpartum Depression (PPD) + Anxiety (PPA) Information **120**

Postpartum Depression + Anxiety Resources **121**

Quick Ways to Calm Down **122**

Organize + Feel Your Feelings Worksheet **123**

Caring for Baby Tips + Tricks **125**

Simple Responses to FAQs + Unsolicited Advice **129**

Sample Daily Schedule (Weeks 1-6) **132**

First Car Seat Checklist **133**

LABOR DAY

Hospital Bag Checklist **136**

Essential Documents for the Hospital Checklist **137**

Diaper Bag Essentials for the Hospital Checklist **138**

Pediatrician Contact Sheet **139**

Baby's Birth Statistics Worksheet. **140**

Questions to Ask the Doctor Before Leaving the Hospital. **141**

Food, Diaper + Sleep Log **146**

ADDITIONAL RESOURCES

Baby's Important Information for Parent(s) **154**

Emergency Information to Leave with Caregiver **155**

Baby's Daily Schedule to Leave with a Caregiver **156**

Medication Tracker **158**

Medical Treatment Authorization **160**

Food, Diaper + Sleep Log **162**

Organize + Feel Your Feelings Worksheet **170**

Notes **176**

References **182**

Acknowledgments **184**

Author Biographies **186**

Thank You **188**

Introduction

Self-help books have been my guide through life for as long as I can remember. During my awkward teenage years, the book *How to Make People Like You in 90 Seconds or Less* about Neurolinguistic Programming was my security blanket. It still gets credit for my first kiss at a sleepaway Economics camp.

Fast forward to my first college semester, and I found myself swept off my feet by Brandon, a funny football player I met tutoring Human Genetics. Confused by this new emotion, I picked up the book *I Love You. Now What?* Fifteen years, five states, one dog, and two kids later, the book still sits on our bookshelf.

When I found out I was pregnant, I could not wait to find my next literal companion. I read several books, but none felt like "the one." Then, once Carter was born, I kept asking myself, "Why did I spend so much time test-driving strollers and reading about when his fingernails grew when I could have spent that time being laser-focused on completing the pregnancy 'need-to-do's' and learning how to prepare for the tsunami of responsibilities that come with motherhood?"

Sleep schedules, hunger cues, how to share the load with Brandon, how to meditate to reduce anxiety...where was that stuff?! I was panic googling my way through the fourth trimester - learning the important things on the go while entirely sleep-deprived. I did not want anyone else to have the same experience. On a mission, I compiled **everything I wished I had known**, printed, 3-hole punched, and shipped binders to all my pregnant friends. I quickly realized that my passion for helping moms-to-be extended far beyond my network. So, I enlisted Brinya, my best mom friend, and we wrote this book just for you.

Stress Less, Pregnant Mom is here to help you through the wild ride of pregnancy. Each section is broken down by trimester with worksheets, information, and checklists to keep you organized and informed at the right time. During your third trimester, spend some time on the Final Preparations section, which will help prepare you for the exciting and exhausting "fourth" trimester.

From your first ultrasound to your first contraction, we will be cheering you on every step of the way.

Michelle Newman

Countdown to Baby

THE WEEK-BY-WEEK MUST-DO CHECKLIST

WEEKS 1-4

☐ Calculate your due date (about 40 weeks from the first day of your last period).

☐ Take a daily prenatal vitamin with folate or folic acid.

☐ Try to drink about ten 8-ounce glasses of water per day.

☐ Familiarize yourself with the foods and drinks you should avoid.

WEEKS 5-8

☐ Schedule the first few appointments with an OB/GYN that accepts your insurance and delivers at your preferred hospital.

☐ Call your health insurance company to inform them of your pregnancy. If you do not have health insurance in the U.S., try healthcare.gov or contact your local health department for free or reduced prenatal care (1-800-311-2229).

☐ Complete the **Family Medical History Worksheet** (p. 27) with your partner (if applicable) and family members in preparation for your first appointment.

☐ Complete the **Medication List Worksheet** (p. 37) before your first appointment.

☐ Familiarize yourself with the optional fetal abnormality tests and screens offered during the first trimester.

☐ Call your dentist to make your next cleaning appointment.

WEEKS 9-12

☐ Locate essential documents for you and your partner. If needed, apply for new copies (e.g., Birth Certificate, Social Security Card, Driver's License, Certified Marriage License).

☐ Decide when you want to tell your employer you're pregnant.

☐ Ask your Human Resources department about the maternity leave policy.

☐ If you and/or your partner's employer does not offer paid leave, research the options for paid and unpaid leave.

WEEKS 13-16

☐ Create a list of recurring expenses you expect once the baby is born.

☐ Start planning medical expenses. Check if you qualify for government assistance.

☐ Start or add a buffer to your emergency savings fund.

- [ ] Interview childcare providers (daycare, nanny). Join a waitlist, if applicable.

- [ ] Consider enrolling in your employer's Dependent Care FSA for childcare expenses.

- [ ] If you would like a doula (trained labor support professional), use the **Questions to Ask a Potential Doula Worksheet** (p. 61) during interviews.

WEEKS 17-20

- [ ] Schedule a breastfeeding class if you plan to try breastfeeding.

- [ ] Schedule a birthing class that caters to your birth preferences.

- [ ] Update your beneficiaries (e.g., 401k/403b, IRA, life insurance).

- [ ] Write or update your will.

WEEKS 21-24

- [ ] Create your baby registry.

- [ ] Decide if you'll have a baby shower. Choose the date, location and guests.

- [ ] If you want maternity and/or newborn photos, book the photographer.

- [ ] Elevate your feet in the evenings to prevent or reduce swelling.

- [ ] Decide if you want to plan a pre-baby getaway vacation.

WEEKS 25-28

- [ ] Ask your doctor about counting kicks. Start tracking baby's activity.

- [ ] Schedule a hospital tour for around 30 weeks.

- [ ] Start filling out your **Birth Preferences Worksheet** (p. 95).

- [ ] Ensure you're up to date on payments with your doctor's office or midwife.

- [ ] Inform your employer that you are pregnant, and state your intentions for taking maternity leave. Note that FMLA requires at least 30 days notice.

- [ ] If your partner is planning to take leave, remind them to inform their employer.

- [ ] If planning to breastfeed, order your breast pump through insurance.

- [ ] Learn about newborn basics: safe sleep, sleep cues, hunger cues, tummy time, sample feed/nap/play "schedules," when to call the pediatrician or 911 about a health concern, and correct car seat installation and buckling.

- [ ] Consider taking a CPR course in person or online.

- [ ] Attend your baby shower (typically between 28-32 weeks).

- [ ] Test smoke and carbon monoxide detectors and replace batteries.

WEEKS 29-32

☐ Interview a pediatrician who accepts your health insurance (p. 90).

☐ Set up the bassinet or crib in your room.

☐ Assemble gear you'll use in the first few months.

☐ Purchase anything left on the registry before your baby's arrival.

☐ Stock up on everyday essentials (toiletries, household supplies, etc.).

☐ Decide who will care for your pets once you go into labor. If your pet will be boarded, ensure they are up to date on shots.

☐ Send baby shower thank you notes.

☐ If your doctor recommends, consider a chiropractor or prenatal massage to alleviate any back pain you may be experiencing.

☐ If your doctor approves, do pelvic floor exercises to strengthen it.

☐ Attend a hospital tour and ask questions (p. 80).

WEEKS 33-36

☐ Sanitize breast pump parts and assemble them to ensure they turn on.

☐ Install the car seat.

☐ Pack hospital bag(s) and baby's diaper bag.

☐ Locate the documents the hospital requires for labor day. Put any documents you don't need daily in a folder in your hospital bag.

☐ Learn about contractions (Braxton Hicks vs. true labor contractions) and how to time them in preparation for labor.

☐ Ask your doctor when you should go to the hospital for labor and if you can eat/drink before coming in.

☐ Review the "Final Preparations" section to ensure you have strategies in place for challenging times postpartum, including how to:

  ○ take care of yourself as a new mom and your new baby
  ○ calm down in an anxious moment
  ○ identify possible symptoms of postpartum depression and anxiety
  ○ reach out for help and support
  ○ organize and feel your feelings
  ○ respond to unsolicited advice

WEEKS 37-40+

☐ Finalize your **Birth Preferences Worksheet** (p. 95), and print a few copies to put a few copies to put in your hospital bag.

☐ Schedule your delivery if it is planned (induction, C-Section, etc.).

☐ Register for delivery with the hospital, if applicable.

☐ Complete the **Pediatrician Contact Sheet** (p. 139).

LABOR DAY + COMING HOME

☐ Complete **Baby's Birth Statistics Worksheet** (p. 140).

☐ Track baby's food, sleep, and diapers.

☐ Complete **Baby's Important Information for Parents** (p. 154) and **Caregivers Worksheets** (p. 155).

Your partner is included in this book because present partners need to be involved and invested in parenthood from day one. If you're single, try to identify a support person(s) who can hold space for you throughout your pregnancy and after your baby arrives.

First Trimester

WEEKS
1-13

I'm Pregnant, Now What?

EARLY FIRST TRIMESTER CHECKLIST

GENERAL

☐ Take a daily prenatal vitamin with folate or folic acid.

☐ Try to drink about ten 8-ounce glasses of water per day.

If you're drinking tap water, order a water test kit to check for contaminants, especially lead, which some filters may not remove.

☐ Familiarize yourself with the foods and drinks you should avoid.

☐ Use an estimated due date calculator, as some providers may not schedule an in-person appointment until you are 8-10 weeks pregnant.

Your estimated due date is typically 40 weeks (280 days) from the first day of your last menstrual period (LMP).

☐ If you are interested in learning in-depth information about your pregnancy, consider reading *What to Expect When You're Expecting* or downloading the WTE app.

DOCTOR, DOCTOR

☐ Schedule the first few appointments with an OB/GYN that accepts your insurance and delivers at your preferred hospital.

☐ Call your health insurance company to inform them of your pregnancy. Start planning medical expenses.

If you do not have health insurance in the U.S., try healthcare.gov and contact your local health department for free or reduced prenatal care (1-800-311-2229).

First day of Last Menstrual Period:

/   /

Ask the doctor the following questions before your appointment:

What can I take for nausea or other symptoms?

_____

_____

Can I continue taking my currently prescribed medications? Can I continue using my over-the-counter medications (e.g., face wash, face cream, pain relievers, etc.)?

_____

_____

Should I take any supplements (choline, fish oil, etc.)?

_____

_____

Are my symptoms typical (e.g., bleeding, throwing up, etc.)? What is considered abnormal to the point where I should call you or visit an emergency room?

_____

_____

_____

How much exercise can/should I be doing?

_____

_____

_____

_____

If you are in an abusive relationship, inform your healthcare provider and put a plan in place for your safety. The **National Domestic Violence Hotline** can be reached by calling **1-800-799-SAFE (7233)** or texting **START** to **88788**.

Survivors of domestic violence can enroll in healthcare insurance at the healthcare. gov website **at any time**, using the Special Enrollment Period (SEP) (National Domestic Violence Hotline, n.d.-b).

If applicable, request support for **quitting alcohol, tobacco, or other substances, and confirm that your job is safe for pregnancy** (e.g., if you are exposed to chemicals, doing heavy lifting, etc.).

First Trimester Checklist

WEEKS 1-13

You're pregnant! If it hasn't sunk in yet, you are not alone. So many emotions are probably running through you. One minute, you're excited, and in the next minute, the excitement may turn to anxiousness. It is normal! These are the things you can do during the first 13 weeks to stay a step ahead of the wild ride to come.

GENERAL

☐ Continue taking a daily prenatal vitamin with folate or folic acid.

☐ Continue drinking plenty of water each day.

☐ Locate important documents for you and your partner. If you don't have them, apply for new copies of your **Birth Certificate, Social Security Card, Driver's License, and Certified Marriage License** (if you've changed your last name).

☐ Get in the habit of going for walks.

☐ Use lotion to avoid dry skin.

☐ Consider a prenatal massage and/or visiting a chiropractor if your doctor approves.

☐ Prioritize rest.

MONEY, HONEY

☐ Decide when to tell your employer you're pregnant, typically after 12 weeks.

☐ Ask your employer's HR department for documentation about the maternity leave policy.

☐ If applicable, remind your partner to ask about their employer's maternity or paternity leave policy.

☐ If your employer(s) do not offer paid maternity or paternity leave, research the options for paid and unpaid leave, such as:

- **FAMILY AND MEDICAL LEAVE ACT OF 1993 (FMLA)**
  - Typically, 12 weeks of **unpaid**, job-protected leave with continuation of group health insurance coverage (U.S. Department of Labor, n.d.).

- **TEMPORARY DISABILITY AND/OR PAID FAMILY LEAVE**
  - Available in some U.S. states.
  - Typically, a percentage of your weekly wage (up to a maximum weekly benefit amount) is **paid** for a certain duration while you care for your baby.

- **PRIVATE SHORT-TERM DISABILITY INSURANCE**
  - Some policies require that you were enrolled before becoming pregnant.
  - Typically, policies pay a percentage of your income for six weeks with a vaginal delivery or eight weeks with a C-section.

- **TIME OFF**
  - Use accrued paid time off, sick days, or a leave of absence.

_____

_____

_____

_____

DOCTOR, DOCTOR

☐ Jot down questions you think can wait until your next appointment.

☐ Complete the **Family Medical History Worksheet** (p. 27) with your partner
☐ (if applicable) and family members in preparation for your first appointment.

☐ Complete the **Medication List Worksheet** (p. 37) before your first appointment.

☐ Call your dentist to make your next cleaning appointment. Pregnant women may be more susceptible to cavities and gum disease and are more likely to develop gingivitis (Centers for Disease Control and Prevention [CDC], 2022b).

☐ Familiarize yourself with the optional fetal abnormality tests and screens offered during the first trimester so that you can **decide which, if any**, you would like performed.

- **First Trimester Screening (American Pregnancy Association, n.d.-a)**
  - Performed between 11 and 14 weeks
  - This screen helps determine the overall risk factor for chromosomal abnormalities such as trisomy 13, 18, or 21. It uses the results of a blood test (hCG and PAPP-A), an ultrasound test for Nuchal Translucency (NT), and maternal age risk factors to determine the risk. Further testing is required for diagnosis.
  - During the ultrasound test for Nuchal Translucency (NT), the back of the baby's neck is checked for increased fluid or skin thickening during an ultrasound, which might indicate a defect.

- **Cell-free DNA Testing: Noninvasive Prenatal Testing (NIPT) and Noninvasive Prenatal Diagnosis (NIPD) (Illinois Department of Public Health [IDPH], 2021)**
  - Performed between 10 and 22 weeks
  - This blood test helps determine the overall risk factor for chromosomal abnormalities such as trisomy 13, 18 or 21,

as well as genetic conditions such as cystic fibrosis or hemophilia. Further testing, however, is required for diagnosis. This test can also tell you the sex of your baby.

- **Chorionic Villus Sampling (CVS) (American Pregnancy Association, n.d.-b)**
  - Performed between 10 and 13 weeks
  - This test looks at a baby's chromosomes using a placenta tissue sample to check for chromosomal abnormalities such as trisomy 18 and 21 or genetic conditions such as cystic fibrosis, sickle cell disease, or Tay-Sachs disease.
  - There are two ways the procedure can be done. In transcervical, the most common method, a catheter is inserted through the cervix into the placenta. In transabdominal, a needle is inserted through the abdomen and uterus into the placenta.

- **Personal Medical History or Genetic-specific testing (Nguyen & Nemours Children's Health, 2022)**
  - cytomegalovirus (CMV)
  - Fragile X syndrome
  - Hepatitis B and C
  - HIV
  - Immunity to rubella
  - Immunity to varicella-zoster virus (chickenpox)
  - Tay-Sachs disease
  - Thyroid disease
  - Toxoplasmosis

If you experience pregnancy loss, help is available.
Contact your OB/GYN to discuss your options for physical and emotional support during this difficult time.

Postpartum Support International offers a helpline (1-800-944-4773) as well as support groups to connect with others who have experienced the pain of pregnancy loss.

Food and Drinks to Avoid

+ COOKING REMINDERS

When you're pregnant, certain foods and drinks are typically off-limits. Review this list and the cooking reminders now because they will apply for the duration of pregnancy. As always, if you have any specific concerns or questions about certain foods or drinks, ask your doctor.

FOOD + DRINKS TO AVOID

According to the U.S. Department of Health & Human Services, food-borne illnesses (e.g., Listeria, E.coli, Salmonella, etc.) can put pregnant women and unborn babies at risk.

The **following foods should be avoided during pregnancy** (U.S. Department of Health & Human Services, 2020):

✗ Raw fish (e.g., sushi, sashimi, raw oysters/clams/scallops, ceviche)

✗ Smoked seafood (e.g., salmon, trout, whitefish, cod, tuna, mackerel, which are often labeled as "Nova-style," "lox," "kippered," "smoked," or "jerky")

✗ Raw milk and any raw milk soft cheeses (e.g., brie, feta, camembert, Roquefort, queso blanco, queso fresco)

✗ Pre-made meat or seafood salads (e.g., prepackaged chicken or seafood salad)

✗ Undercooked meat and poultry

✗ Hot dogs, deli meats, cold cuts

✗ Fermented or dry sausage

✗ Refrigerated meat spreads, pâtés

✗ Raw sprouts

✗ Uncooked/undercooked eggs (e.g., over easy/medium, eggs benedict, raw batter or dough, homemade Caesar salad dressing, tiramisu, homemade hollandaise sauce, homemade eggnog)

✗ Fish with high mercury levels (e.g., King mackerel, marlin, orange roughy, shark, swordfish, tilefish, albacore/yellowfin/bigeye tuna)

✗ Avoid unpasteurized/fresh-squeezed juice or cider unless you bring it to a rolling boil and continue boiling for at least one minute before drinking.

✗ Alcohol

✗ Consider limiting caffeinated drinks to less than 200mg daily (e.g., 12 ounces of coffee), or eliminating them (March of Dimes, 2020).

FOOD PREPARATION + COOKING REMINDERS

- If you still have the energy to grocery shop (hello grocery delivery!) and cook while pregnant, you're an all-star in our book. Just keep these protocols in mind, which the U.S. Food and Drug Administration (2022) recommends.
- Keep your refrigerator temperature to 40°F or below and your freezer to 0°F or below.

Use an appliance thermometer if your appliances don't have digital thermometers.

- Store raw meat, poultry, and seafood in a sealed container or securely wrapped in the refrigerator or freezer.
- Always use a food thermometer to make sure whatever you cook has reached a minimum safe internal temperature, which varies based on the food.

- It's best to skip over-easy and over-medium eggs during pregnancy in favor of scrambled or over-hard eggs.
- Sprouts should be cooked thoroughly rather than eaten raw.
- The CDC (2023b) recommends freezing meat for a few days at sub-zero temperatures before cooking and always cooking it to the USDA-recommended minimum safe internal temperature to reduce the risk of contracting Toxoplasmosis.
- The internal temperature for cooking meats such as beef, veal, lamb, and pork can vary based on the cut and the rest time (the amount of time the food remains at the final temperature after removing it from the grill, oven, etc.).
- Wash your hands with soap and warm running water for at least 20 seconds.
- Wash all fresh fruits and vegetables, including salads, under running water.
- Wash everything that comes into contact with raw meat, poultry, seafood, unwashed fruits/vegetables, flour, and raw dough (e.g., dishes, counters, utensils, cutting boards, food thermometers, etc.).

When using a food thermometer, put it into the **thickest part of the food** (avoiding bone, fat, gristle).

Check the temperature closer to the end of cooking, but before you think it's done.

165°F

RECOMMENDED MINIMUM INTERNAL TEMPERATURE (U.S. DEPARTMENT OF AGRICULTURE [USDA], 2020):

165°F — **Poultry (including ground turkey/chicken), leftovers, casseroles**

- To reduce the risk of Listeria, reheat hot dogs, lunch meats, and deli meats to 165°F, which is steaming hot, before eating.

- Smoked seafood can be eaten if it's canned, shelf-stable, or an ingredient in a dish cooked to 165°F.

160°F — **Ground meat (excluding ground poultry), eggs**

145°F — **With at least three minutes of rest time: Beef, pork, veal, lamb, steaks, chops, roasts, ham (fresh or smoked)**

145°F — **Fish, shellfish**

Medical History + Questions

Your first prenatal appointment, usually between 6 and 10 weeks, makes pregnancy feel oh-so-real. This appointment is jam-packed, from bloodwork and a pap smear to finding out your due date and possibly seeing your baby for the first time via an ultrasound. With all the excitement, it can be hard to remember to ask all the questions you've had floating in your head since you saw your positive pregnancy test. This list will prepare you for what your OB/GYN will likely ask you and what you should consider asking at your first prenatal visit.

QUESTIONS YOUR DOCTOR MAY ASK YOU:

- **Your medical history:** Complete the *Medical History Worksheet* (p. 27) to note if you've had any medical issues in the past (e.g., cancer, diabetes, high blood pressure, epilepsy, kidney disease, abnormal pap smears, anxiety, depression, etc.). Plan to discuss them with your doctor. Gather any documents that pertain to your medical history, if applicable.

- **Family medical history (you + father):** Have a conversation with the father, if applicable, about his family's medical history. Were there any genetic disorders or congenital disabilities? Consider the same for your own family's medical history.

- **Your gynecological history:** When was your last period? What are your periods like (regular/irregular, cramping, PMS)? Which, if any, STDs have you had? When?

- **Fertility treatments:** Which, if any, fertility treatments have you used?

- **History of previous pregnancy:** Have you ever been pregnant before?

- **Medications:** Complete the *Medication List Worksheet* (p. 37) to note the medications you take or use, including those that are occasional and/or over-the-counter (e.g., ibuprofen, acetaminophen, cortisone, medicated face washes, etc.).

- **Diet:** Be prepared to answer questions about your caffeine, alcohol, and nicotine consumption. If you have any substance addictions (alcohol, tobacco, etc.), seek help and make a plan to quit.

Medical History Worksheet

MY GENERAL HEALTH HISTORY:

Age: _____   Weight (pre-pregnancy): _____

Ethnicity: _____   Blood type: _____

Allergies (food, medication, etc.):

_____

_____

Health conditions:

_____

_____

_____

Previous surgeries:

_____

_____

Primary care physician name and phone number:

_____

_____

Were you vaccinated against?

Measles, mumps, rubella (MMR):	☐ Yes	☐ No
Varicella (chickenpox):	☐ Yes	☐ No
Human Papillomavirus (HPV):	☐ Yes	☐ No
Tetanus, Diphtheria, Pertussis (TDAP):	☐ Yes	☐ No
Seasonal influenza (Flu):	☐ Yes	☐ No
COVID-19:	☐ Yes	☐ No

If you are unsure about your vaccination status, contact your primary care physician.

GYNECOLOGICAL HEALTH HISTORY:

Age at first period: _____

First day of last menstrual period: _____

Average length of menstrual cycle: _____ days

Date of last Pap smear: _____ / _____ / _____ ☐ NORMAL ☐ ABNORMAL

Have you had any abnormal Pap smears? If so, which, if any, treatment did you receive?

_____

_____

_____

_____

Last birth control method(s) used?

_____

Do you have any gynecological conditions (e.g., bleeding between menstrual cycles, irregular or non-existent periods, polycystic ovary syndrome, etc.)?

_____

_____

_____

_____

Have you had a sexually transmitted disease (STD)? If so, which one(s) and when? Did you receive treatment?

_____

_____

_____

REPRODUCTIVE HEALTH HISTORY:

Have you been pregnant before? If so, how many times?

_____

_____

Have you ever had an/an:

Miscarriage:	☐ Yes	☐ No	Other:	_____
Ectopic pregnancy:	☐ Yes	☐ No		_____
Abortion:	☐ Yes	☐ No		_____
Stillbirth:	☐ Yes	☐ No		_____

If yes, how many and when? How many weeks along were you?

_____

_____

_____

Before conceiving, did you receive any fertility assistance (e.g., hormone injections, intrauterine insemination (IUI), in vitro fertilization (IVF), donor egg transfer, egg freezing, etc.)?

_____

_____

_____

_____

ADDITIONAL NOTES

_____

_____

ADDITIONAL HEALTH HISTORY:

Do you:

Smoke cigarettes:	☐ Yes	☐ No
Smoke marijuana:	☐ Yes	☐ No
Drink alcohol:	☐ Yes	☐ No
Use illicit drugs:	☐ Yes	☐ No
Drink caffeine (e.g., coffee, soda):	☐ Yes	☐ No
Exercise:	☐ Yes	☐ No
Own a cat:	☐ Yes	☐ No
Perform heavy lifting at work:	☐ Yes	☐ No
Stand for long hours at work:	☐ Yes	☐ No
Feel unsafe at work:	☐ Yes	☐ No
Feel unsafe at home:	☐ Yes	☐ No
Feel depressed:	☐ Yes	☐ No
Feel anxious:	☐ Yes	☐ No

ADDITIONAL NOTES

_____

_____

_____

_____

_____

_____

PARTNER'S HEALTH HISTORY:

Age: _____   Weight: _____

Ethnicity: _____   Blood type: _____

Does your partner:

Smoke cigarettes: ☐ **Yes**   ☐ **No**

Smoke marijuana: ☐ **Yes**   ☐ **No**

Drink alcohol: ☐ **Yes**   ☐ **No**

Use illicit drugs: ☐ **Yes**   ☐ **No**

If applicable, get support for quitting tobacco or illicit drugs.

ADDITIONAL NOTES

_____

_____

_____

_____

_____

_____

_____

_____

_____

_____

_____

MEDICAL CONDITION	ME OR MY FAMILY	PARTNER OR PARTNER'S FAMILY	NOTES
A or B-thalessemia			
Allergies			
Arthritis			
Asthma			
Autism			
Autoimmune Disorders			
Blood Transfusions			
Breast Cancer			
Bronchitis			
Colon Cancer			
Cystic Fibrosis			
Depression			
Diabetes			
Down Syndrome			
Eating Disorder			
Emphysema			
Endometrial Cancer			
Epilepsy (Seizures)			
Gallstones			
Hearing Loss			
Heart Disease			
Hemophilia or other Coagulation Abnormality			

MEDICAL CONDITION	ME OR MY FAMILY	PARTNER OR PARTNER'S FAMILY	NOTES
High Blood Pressure			
HIV+			
Huntington's Chorea			
Kidney Disease			
Liver Disease (incl. Hepatitis)			
Muscular Dystrophy			
Neural Tube Defects (Spina Bifida, Anencephaly, etc.)			
Neurological Disorders			
Other Chromosomal Abnormality			
Other Genetic Disorder			
Ovarian Cancer			
Phenylketonuria (PKU)			
Preeclampsia			
Psychiatric Disorders			
Recurrent Miscarriage			
Sickle-cell Disease			
Stillbirths			
Tay-Sachs Disease			
Thyroid Disease			

Questions to Ask Your OB/GYN

DOCTOR: _____ DATE: ____/____/____

What should I look for in a prenatal vitamin? Do you recommend a brand?

_____

_____

Do you have advice for combating early pregnancy symptoms (nausea, vomiting, fatigue, etc)? Vitamin B6, ginger tablets, etc.?

_____

_____

Can I continue taking my prescribed medications? Are there any I should avoid?

_____

_____

Can I continue taking my over-the-counter medications (e.g., face wash, face cream, pain relievers, etc.)? Are there any I should avoid?

_____

_____

Should I take any supplements (choline, fish oil, etc)?

_____

_____

How much exercise can/should I be doing?

_____

_____

How much caffeine can I drink? Should I change my current intake?

_____

Throughout pregnancy, when should I call or go into the hospital (e.g., bleeding, cramping, feeling faint)?

_____

_____

What is my estimated due date? _____

When is my next appointment? _____

When is my next ultrasound? _____

Can my partner come to the appointments? Ultrasounds?

_____

_____

Which, if any, prenatal screening or testing do you recommend?

_____

_____

Which, if any, birth and/or parenting classes do you recommend? When should I take them?

_____

_____

Is my pregnancy considered high-risk? If so, what exactly does that mean?

_____

_____

What does a healthy weight gain look like for me?

_____

_____

Which vaccines do you recommend I receive during pregnancy?
What is the timeline for them?

_____

_____

ADDITIONAL CONSIDERATIONS:

Can you tell me about your experience working with patients of color?
What have their birth outcomes been?

_____

_____

_____

What is my risk for preeclampsia and other complications?

_____

_____

Do you have any strategies for overcoming the current Black maternal
mortality statistics?

_____

_____

Can you tell me about your experience working with overweight patients?
What have their birth outcomes been?

_____

_____

Can you tell me about your experience working with patients with disordered
eating or eating disorders? What have their birth outcomes been?

_____

_____

ADDITIONAL NOTES

_____

_____

Remember, if you are
in an abusive relationship,
please inform your healthcare
provider and put a plan in place
for your safety. The **National
Domestic Violence Hotline** can
be reached by calling **1-800-799-
SAFE (7233)** or by texting **START**
to **88788** (National Domestic
Violence Hotline, n.d.-a).

Medication List

PHARMACY: _____

PHONE # _____

ADDRESS: _____

MEDICATION	DOSE	FREQUENCY	PRESCRIBING DOCTOR OR OVER-THE-COUNTER

ADDITIONAL NOTES

_____

_____

Maternity Leave Request Emails

+ OTHER TEMPLATES

When you're pregnant, your to-do list feels endless — endless appointments, endless paperwork, endless thank-you notes—all while juggling work and relationships and trying to appear "perky" when you can barely remember the last time you slept well!

When the time comes to request maternity leave from your employer, it can feel scary, even when it's the absolute LEAST they can do for us as we prolong the existence of the human race. To make your life a little easier, we're sharing some templates you can use for telling your boss you're pregnant, requesting maternity leave, and even asking for a leave of absence if you don't feel ready to go back when the time comes.

Telling Your Boss You're Pregnant

When to send: Typically at the end of the first trimester or early second

Subject: Quick Catch Up

Body:

Hi [Manager's Name],
I wanted to share that I'm pregnant and am due in [month of due date]. I know we have a lot of work to do between now and then, so I wanted to put this on your radar sooner rather than later. Once we get closer to the due date, I'd love to come up with a plan for coverage during my maternity leave. I plan on telling the rest of the team sometime soon!

Thank you,
[Your Name]

Request for Maternity Leave Documentation

When to send: Anytime

Subject: Maternity Leave Policy

Body:

Hi [HR Representative's Name],
Can you please share the documentation related to our maternity leave policy?

Thank you,
[Your Name]

Telling Your Clients You're Pregnant

When to send: Typically at the end of the second trimester or early third

Subject: Personal News

Body:

Hi [Client's Name],
I wanted to share that I'm pregnant and am due in [month of due date]. I am planning to take maternity leave for [x weeks/months] from [date] to [date], but the beginning date may vary based on baby's arrival. Until then, I will continue working with you and will prepare my colleagues to work with you in my absence. I know we have a lot of work to do between now and then, so I wanted to put this on your radar sooner rather than later. Once we get closer to the due date, I will be happy to discuss specific logistics around coverage during my maternity leave.

Thank you,
[Your Name]

Maternity Leave Request to HR

When to send: Typically by the end of the second trimester, but at least 30 days before the due date if your company is subject to FMLA

Subject: Maternity Leave Request

Body:

Hi [HR Person's Name],
I am pregnant and would like to take maternity leave upon the baby's arrival. My due date is [date], and I plan to continue working until [date]. Per our leave policy, I plan to take [x weeks/months] of maternity leave, and then I anticipate resuming my current position. While I am on leave, [Colleague's Name] will be the point of contact for my duties. I have already worked out the details with [Colleague] and [Manager's Name]. I can be contacted via [personal email address] or [cell phone number] while I'm on leave if necessary. Please let me know if you need any additional information from me before then or any documentation you may need after the baby is born.

I appreciate your support during my transition to maternity leave and eventual return to work. If anything changes, I will be sure to let you know.

Thank you,
[Your Name]

Maternity Leave Out of Office (OOO)

When to set your calendar as OOO: Your first day of leave, if it's before you go into labor. If not, once you're home from the hospital and have a minute to log in.

Subject: Out of Office

Body:

Thank you for your email. I am out of the office on maternity leave until [MM/DD/YY]. For any questions related to [subject matter], please contact [colleague's email address].

Thank you,
[Your Name]

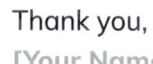

Leave of Absence Request
(Extend Maternity Leave)

When to send: If you don't think you'll be ready to return to work after maternity leave, you may be able to ask for a leave of absence. Asking as soon as you think you may need more time will give you the best chance for a smooth transition from maternity leave to an LOA. Research the pros and cons of a leave of absence before requesting one.

Subject: Leave of Absence Request

Body:

Hi [HR Representative's Name],
I am currently on maternity leave, and it is scheduled
to end [MM/DD/YY]. I was wondering if it is possible to take a leave of absence
so that I can continue taking care of my infant [and/or personal recovery]. If so,
can you please share the details or documentation of our leave of absence policy?

Thank you,
[Your Name]

Returning from Maternity Leave

When to send: Once you return to work from maternity leave, confirm it with HR so you can reinstate your income and benefits, if applicable. It may make the transition more manageable if you let people know slowly. Tell the people who need to know first (HR, your manager, any direct reports, etc.), then inform others.

Subject: Returning from Maternity Leave

Body:

Hi [HR Representative's Name],
I have returned from maternity leave as of [date]. Please let me know if you need anything from me to be reinstated as a full-time employee.

Thank you,
[Your Name]

My Prenatal Appointments

TYPICAL APPOINTMENT SCHEDULE:

WEEKS 4-28: 1 PER MONTH

WEEKS 28-36: 1 EVERY 2 WEEKS

WEEKS 36-40+: 1 PER WEEK

DATE	TIME	WEEK	DOCTOR

First Ultrasound

DATE: _____

ADDITIONAL NOTES

_____
_____
_____
_____
_____
_____

Second Trimester

WEEKS

14-27

Second Trimester Checklist

You're 14 weeks in—congratulations! In honor of (hopefully) reduced morning sickness and increased energy levels, these are the things you can do during the second trimester to prepare for baby's arrival.

GENERAL

☐ Continue taking a daily prenatal vitamin with folate or folic acid and drinking plenty of water.

☐ Consider taking a breastfeeding class if you plan to try breastfeeding.

☐ Consider taking a birthing class that caters to your intended birth plan.

☐ Locate the documents you will need on labor day, or apply for new copies.

☐ Create your baby registry.

☐ Start organizing any baby items you've purchased or received as a gift.

☐ Wash clothes/bedding in baby-safe detergent. Store baby clothes by size.

☐ Interview childcare providers (daycare, nanny). Join a waitlist, if applicable.

☐ Decide if you'll have a baby shower. Choose a date, location, and guests.

☐ Decide if you want maternity and/or newborn photos. If so, book a photographer.

☐ Research cord blood banking. Decide if you will bank your baby's umbilical cord blood.

☐ Elevate your feet in the evenings to prevent or reduce swelling.

☐ Decide if you want to plan a pre-baby vacation. Whether it's an extravagant trip to Cabo or a special weekend staycation, you'll always think back fondly on the times you took to sleep in and eat a meal in peace.

DOCTOR, DOCTOR

☐ Schedule a hospital tour.

☐ Start filling out your **Birth Preferences Worksheet** (p. 95).

☐ If you would like a doula (a trained labor support professional), use the **Questions to Ask a Potential Doula Worksheet** (p. 61) during the interviews.

_____

_____

_____

_____

MONEY, HONEY

☐ Make sure you're up to date on payments with your doctor's office, midwife, and doula.

☐ Inform your employer that you are pregnant. State your intentions for taking maternity leave. Note that FMLA requires at least 30 days notice.

☐ If your partner is planning to take leave, remind them to inform their employer.

☐ Draft a list of recurring expenses you expect once your baby is born.

☐ Start or add a buffer to your emergency savings fund (~3-6 months living expenses).

☐ Write or update your will.

☐ Consider enrolling in your employer's Dependent Care FSA if you will incur childcare expenses.

☐ Update your beneficiaries (e.g., 401k/403b, IRA, life insurance).

☐ If applicable, check if you qualify for financial assistance during pregnancy and postpartum (WIC, Medicaid, single-mother-grants).

Baby Registry Checklist

WEEKS 14-27

NURSERY

- [ ] Bassinet
- [ ] Bassinet sheets (1-2)
- [ ] Crib
- [ ] Crib mattress
- [ ] Crib mattress waterproof cover
- [ ] Crib sheets (2-3)
- [ ] Sound machine
- [ ] Baby monitor/camera
- [ ] Hamper
- [ ] Dresser
- [ ] Blackout curtains
- [ ] Rocking chair/glider
- [ ] Changing/side table
- [ ] Hangers

CLOTHING

- [ ] Alternative gown for labor
- [ ] Hat + mittens for hospital (NB)
- [ ] Coming home outfit (NB)
- [ ] Swaddles (0-3M)
- [ ] 2-way zipper-footed PJs (NB-12M)
- [ ] Onesies (NB-12M)
- [ ] Socks (0-12M)
- [ ] Pants, leggings, sweatpants
- [ ] Shorts
- [ ] Sweatshirt, jacket
- [ ] Sleep Sack (3M+)
- [ ] Booties (size 1, 2)
- [ ] Shoes (size 3+)
- [ ] Reusable swim diaper
- [ ] Swimsuit

GEAR

- [ ] Car seat
- [ ] Stroller
- [ ] Stroller organizer
- [ ] Pacifiers
- [ ] Blankets
- [ ] Pacifier clips
- [ ] Diaper bag
- [ ] Ergonomic baby carrier or sling
- [ ] Car mirror
- [ ] Portable sound machine
- [ ] Pack n' Play

Review safe usage guidelines from the AAP for the following:

- [ ] Swing
- [ ] Newborn lounger
- [ ] Bouncer

CHANGING

- [ ] Changing pad
- [ ] Changing pad cover
- [ ] Changing pad for the diaper bag
- [ ] Diapers
- [ ] Baby wipes
- [ ] Diaper rash ointment/cream
- [ ] Diaper cream applicator
- [ ] Wet/dry bags
- [ ] Diaper pail
- [ ] Diaper pail bag refills
- [ ] Disposable diaper bags
- [ ] Laundry detergent

FEEDING (*Breastfeeding, +Formula)

- [ ] *Nursing bras
- [ ] *Nursing pads
- [ ] *Lanolin nipple cream
- [ ] *Nursing pillow
- [ ] *Hot/cold breast therapy gel packs
- [ ] *Silver nursing cups
- [ ] *Double breast pump (likely available for free through your insurance)
- [ ] *Silicone breast pump
- [ ] *Silicone milk collector
- [ ] *Hands-free pumping bra (if your pump is not wireless)
- [ ] *Milk storage bags
- [ ] +Formula
- [ ] +Formula dispenser/mixer
- [ ] +Formula travel dispenser
- [ ] Bottles
- [ ] Bottle warmer
- [ ] Bottle sterilizer
- [ ] Microwaveable sterilizer bag
- [ ] Drying rack
- [ ] Burp cloths
- [ ] Baby dish soap
- [ ] Dishwasher basket

INTRODUCING SOLIDS

- [ ] Bibs
- [ ] Plates
- [ ] Bowls
- [ ] Open cups
- [ ] Straw cups
- [ ] Silverware (spoons, forks)
- [ ] Silicone placemat
- [ ] High chair

HEALTH/SAFETY

- [ ] Gas drops
- [ ] *Vitamin D drops
- [ ] Probiotic drops
- [ ] First aid kit
- [ ] Nail clippers + file
- [ ] Baby hair brush
- [ ] Gas/constipation reliever
- [ ] Nasal aspirator + saline
- [ ] Cool-mist humidifier
- [ ] Thermometer
- [ ] Hand sanitizer
- [ ] Toothbrush
- [ ] Infant acetaminophen (check with baby's pediatrician)
- [ ] Spare batteries for smoke detector
- [ ] Spare batteries for carbon monoxide detector
- [ ] Fire extinguisher
- [ ] Portable carbon monoxide detector

CHILDPROOFING

- [ ] Baby gate(s)
- [ ] Outlet covers
- [ ] Drawer latches/cabinet locks
- [ ] Door knob covers
- [ ] Stove knob covers
- [ ] Anti-tip furniture anchors
- [ ] Anti-tip TV straps
- [ ] Corner guards
- [ ] Toilet locks
- [ ] Blind cord holder

If Applicable:

- [ ] Pool fence + alarm
- [ ] Fireplace gate
- [ ] Window lock/guards/stoppers
- [ ] Stair bannister guard

BATH

- [ ] Bathtub
- [ ] Washcloths
- [ ] Baby soap/shampoo
- [ ] Baby lotion
- [ ] Towels (hooded)
- [ ] Bath kneeler + elbow pad
- [ ] Water thermometer
- [ ] Rinser
- [ ] Bathtub spout cover
- [ ] Non-slip bath mat
- [ ] Mold-free bath toys

ACTIVITY

- [ ] Board books
- [ ] Crinkle books
- [ ] Stuffed animal(s)
- [ ] Activity mat
- [ ] Teethers
- [ ] Rattle
- [ ] Ring stacker
- [ ] Blocks
- [ ] Baby's first-year memory book
- [ ] Month blanket for photos

EDUCATIONAL CLASSES

- [ ] Infant CPR + choking
- [ ] Labor + birthing techniques
- [ ] Postpartum preparation + healing
- [ ] Breastfeeding + lactation
- [ ] Baby care
- [ ] Newborn sleep course (e.g., Taking Cara Babies, Moms on Call)
- [ ] Introducing solids (e.g., Solid Starts, Feeding Littles)

THINGS WE SKIPPED OR USED VERY MINIMALLY

- Infant bathtub for sink
- Separate changing table
- Bottle brush
- Vehicle trunk changing system
- Specific nose/pacifier wipes
- Pacifier medicine dispenser
- Gripe water
- Bath caddy
- Baby bathrobe
- Wipes warmer
- Baby food processor/blender
- Bouncers: According to the AAP, "excessive time in these devices inhibits movement and places babies at higher risk for a variety of issues, such as plagiocephaly, decreased strength, and delayed motor milestones (LaBotz, 2020).
- Jumpers, contained activity centers ("Exersaucer"), or floor booster seats: It is recommended to keep usage of containers to a maximum of 15 minutes twice a day to avoid hip dysplasia (Children's Rehabilitation Institute TeletonUSA, 2020).

DUE TO SAFETY CONCERNS, WE DID NOT USE:

- **Infant Walkers**

  - The American Academy of Pediatrics (2022b) has called for a ban on their manufacture and sale in the United States due to the risk of injury.

- **Crib Bumpers and Inclined Sleepers**

  - Crib bumpers pose a suffocation risk, entrapment, and strangulation (DiMaggio & American Academy of Pediatrics [AAP], 2023).

  - Inclined sleepers and sleep positioners also pose a suffocation risk. As of 2023, inclined sleepers have been associated with at least 94 infant deaths (DiMaggio & AAP, 2023).

  - The Safe Sleep for Babies Act of 2021 "makes it unlawful to manufacture, sell, or distribute crib bumpers or inclined sleepers for infants. Specifically, inclined sleepers for infants are those designed for an infant up to one year old and have an inclined sleep surface of greater than 10 degrees. Crib bumpers generally are padded materials inserted around the inside of a crib and intended to prevent the crib occupant from becoming trapped in any part of the crib's openings" (*Safe Sleep for Babies Act of 2021*, 2021).

- **Bath Squirting Toys**

  - Soft, flexible plastic bath toys with holes retain water even after they are squeezed out, making it easy for mold and mildew to grow inside (Bhaskar, 2021).

Things You Can Likely Buy Second-hand

REMINDER: Check with the Consumer Product Safety Commission to find out if a particular item has been recalled before buying it second-hand.

https://www.cpsc.gov/Recalls

- Baby carrier or sling
- Swing
- Bouncer
- Stroller
- High chair
- Changing table/dresser
- Diaper pail
- Bassinet, Crib, Pack n' Play
- Clothes
- Infant bathtub
- Sound machine
- Books

If it is in your budget, consider hiring a "**newborn care specialist**" to help you for the first few weeks at home.

They typically work overnight, giving new moms much-needed time to rest.

Monthly Budget for Baby

PRODUCT	DESCRIPTION	COST/MONTH
DIAPERS		
BABY WIPES		
CHILDCARE		
FEEDING SUPPLIES	Milk collection/storage, spare pump parts, formula	
CLOTHING		
BABY GEAR		
TOYS/BOOKS		
PRENATAL VITAMINS		
UTILITIES	Increased usage: water/electricity	
	TOTAL	

If you plan to use childcare once your baby arrives, research the local rates for your preferred option to estimate the monthly cost.

Baby Registry 101

While preparing for our first babies, we did a lot of research regarding baby registries and which "must-haves" and brands to add to our checklists. However, once our babies were here, we found we had spent too much time on "what" rather than "when" and "why." After you've had fun test-driving strollers and reading every review for your baby's first hooded bath towel (okay, maybe we went overboard!), take some time to learn about how you'll use the baby items you're adding to your cart.

WHAT YOU'LL USE AND WHEN YOU'LL USE IT

BASSINET

- Typically used for the first three to four months, but can be used for as long as 5 or 6 months depending on factors such as your baby's size, the bassinet's size, and when your baby begins rolling over or pulling up.
- Note that while you can start your baby out from day one in a crib or specific sleep-approved pack 'n plays, the bassinet can be convenient for a few reasons. First, it is usually quite high off the ground, so you won't need to bend too far down to place your baby in. Second, it is relatively small, so it can be close to your bed, which may make night feedings and changes easier.
- The AAP (2022a) recommends sleeping in the same room (but not the same bed) for the first six months. So, if you don't have the nursery set up or you don't have a spare room, that's okay!

SWADDLES FOR SLEEP

- Typically used for the first two to three months. You must stop swaddling once baby attempts to roll over.
- Keep in mind that improper swaddling may lead to hip dysplasia.

  - To avoid hip dysplasia, the International Hip Dysplasia Institute recommends that legs be able to bend up and out at the hips, allowing for natural development of the hip joints. In other words, the baby's legs should not be tightly wrapped straight down and pressed together (International Hip Dysplasia Institute, 2020).

STROLLER

- Typically used until your baby is 2-3 years old, but it will depend on the stroller's weight limit (and your toddler's mood that day!).
- Some strollers offer compatibility with certain infant car seats. Check if a separate piece (adapter) is required to purchase or if it is compatible as-is.
- The ability to remove the stroller seat

and click the car seat into the stroller can be convenient for going from the car to errands, appointments, or walks.

- **Stroller Bassinet Attachment**
  - Bassinets are ideal for newborns and babies without the neck support and muscle tone to sit upright for a long time. Some strollers offer these as an attachment, and other stroller seats can be tilted back to be completely flat.

- **Double Strollers**
  - If you plan to have babies back to back (or are expecting multiples), you may want to consider a stroller that can handle more than one little one at a time.

CAR SEAT:

- According to the AAP (2023), "Children should ride in a **rear-facing car safety seat as long as possible, up to the limits of their car safety seat. This will include virtually all children under 2 years of age and most children up to age 4**."
- Typically, you will buy two car seats: a rear-facing infant car seat and a convertible car seat. The convertible car seat should remain rear-facing until your baby reaches the rear-facing height and weight limits, at which point you will face it forward.

- **Rear-facing infant car seat:** Approximately 0 to 9 months, depending on the car seat's height and weight limits.

- **Convertible car seat:** Can be installed **rear-facing** and used from day one. Typically used closer to 9 months through age 4 or older, depending on the car seat's height and weight limits.

- Immediately register your car seat with the manufacturer to be notified in the case of a safety recall.
- Don't install your car seat too early. If you get into an accident before your baby arrives, you may have to replace the car seat. Your automobile insurance will often replace it, but this can take some time.
- Car seats have expiration dates, so be sure to consider this if you buy a car seat second-hand or want to use it for future babies.
- Your instruction manual will explain how to install the car seat. Check for the manufacturer's videos online as well.
- You can also have your car seat installation inspected by certified technicians free of charge. Find a place near you using the NHTSA website.

  https://www.nhtsa.gov

- Read your car seat's manual to learn how to buckle your baby in properly.

HIGH CHAIR:

- Typically used from approximately 4 months to 18-24 months.
- Some high chairs have a "recline" setting that can be used earlier than four months for sitting/bottle feeding but not for eating solids. Solid foods will start closer to 4-6 months, depending on your pediatrician's recommendation.
- Once you start feeding solids, the baby needs to be in an upright position, ideally with a well-positioned footrest.
- Register your high chair with the manufacturer after you buy it to be notified in the case of a safety recall.
- If you use a second-hand high chair, check the Consumer Product Safety Commission website to see if it has been recalled.

  https://www.cpsc.gov/Recalls

- Before choosing a high chair, read reviews online about whether it's easy to clean, sturdy, and comfortable!
- To keep your baby safe in the high chair, **always**:

  o use the safety straps
  o make sure the chair is stable
  o stay with your baby when they are seated

- **Introducing Solids to Your Baby:**
  o Purées: If you and your pediatrician decide to start your baby with purées, you'll likely start using the specific feeding items (spoons, bibs, baby food, high chair) between 4 and 6 months.
  o Baby-led weaning: If you and your pediatrician decide to follow the baby-led weaning route, you'll likely start using the items (self-feeding spoons, plates, bowls, open cup, straw cup, bibs, high chair) around 6 months when your baby can sit independently.

BOUNCERS, SWINGS, ETC.:

- Typically used from 0-4 months, depending on the item's weight and height limits.
- Make sure baby's chin is not touching their chest, as it can block the airway. The head positioned to the side is natural and better for breathing.
- Avoid prolonged use of containers like bouncers and swings to avoid "flat head syndrome."
- If you think your baby's head appears flat, talk to your pediatrician. They may recommend physical therapy and/or a helmet.

NEWBORN SLEEP TIPS

- We recommend the Taking Cara Babies Newborn course. She will teach you so much about how to survive the early days with your baby. From sleep and hunger cues to wake windows and feeding routines, you'll feel far more confident going into parenthood, having taken her course.

BIRTH CLASS

- While it's not something you will register for, you may want to set aside money for a birth class. The hospital may offer a free class, but it doesn't hurt to research the type of class that fits you best.
- For example, are you planning to ask for an epidural, are you hoping to have an unmedicated birth, or will you be having a C-Section? Do you plan to give birth in a hospital or birthing center? Is your partner going to be present, or are you laboring solo? Having a general idea of your birth plan may help you decide which type of birth class to take.

SELF-CARE + LOOSE ENDS

- Take time to pamper yourself and tie up loose ends before baby comes.
- Anything you can take off your plate for the first month or two will be worth the hassle now. Could you use a haircut or color? Book it! Do you have a couple of minutes to paint your toenails? Now's the time! Have you been putting off taking your dog to the vet to update shots or doing the overnight trial run at doggie daycare? Here's your sign! Does your car need an oil change? *You get the idea.*
- Keep your gas tank **3/4 full** during the third trimester, just in case!
- Make one last big trip to Costco or Target to stock up on essentials.
- Swap some late-night social media scrolling for reading or thinking about:

  o How to identify postpartum depression and anxiety and what resources to utilize
  o Ways to take care of yourself as a new mom
  o If applicable, how you and your partner will split up household chores

WAYS TO SAVE

- Buy second-hand on Facebook Marketplace, Once Upon a Child, Craigslist, or Goodwill.
- **REMINDER:** Check with the Consumer Product Safety Commission if a particular item has been recalled before buying it second-hand.

https://www.cpsc.gov/Recalls

SPREAD OUT THE PURCHASES:

- You likely won't use the following items in the first three months, so you can buy them later if you would like to spread out your costs.

  o High chair, spoons, plates, bibs, teethers
  o Toys, bath toys
  o Crib/mattress/sheets/pack 'n play (if using a bassinet at first)
  o Babyproofing items
  o Convertible car seat (if planning to buy an infant car seat)
  o Baby monitor (if planning to room share for the first few months)

HEALTH + SAFETY REMINDERS

- **Bouncers:** According to the AAP, "excessive time in these devices inhibits movement and places babies at higher risk for a variety of issues, such as plagiocephaly, decreased strength, and delayed motor milestones (LaBotz, 2020).

- **Jumpers, contained activity centers ("Exersaucer"), floor booster seats:** It is recommended to keep usage of containers to a maximum of 15 minutes twice a day to avoid hip dysplasia (Children's Rehabilitation Institute TeletonUSA, 2020).

- **Squirting bath toys:** Soft, flexible plastic bath toys with holes retain water even after being squeezed out, making it easy for mold and mildew to grow inside (Bhaskar, 2021).

- **Infant walkers:** The American Academy of Pediatrics (2022b) has called for a ban on their manufacture and sale in the United States due to the risk of injury.

- **Crib bumpers and inclined sleepers:**

  - Crib bumpers pose a risk of suffocation, entrapment, and strangulation. As of 2023, they have been linked to more than 100 infant deaths (DiMaggio & American Academy of Pediatrics [AAP], 2023).
  - Mesh bumpers and vertical crib liners also pose a strangulation risk (DiMaggio & American Academy of Pediatrics [AAP], 2023).
  - Inclined sleepers and sleep positioners pose a suffocation risk. As of 2023, inclined sleepers have been associated with at least 94 infant deaths (DiMaggio & AAP, 2023).

  - The Safe Sleep for Babies Act of 2021 "makes it **unlawful to manufacture, sell, or distribute crib bumpers or inclined sleepers** for infants. Specifically, inclined sleepers for infants are those designed for an infant up to one year old and have an inclined sleep surface of greater than 10 degrees. Crib bumpers generally are padded materials inserted around the inside of a crib and intended to prevent the crib occupant from becoming trapped in any part of the crib's openings" (*Safe Sleep for Babies Act of 2021*, 2021).

Sharing the Load

When we become new mothers, we often assume the role of "default parent." From middle-of-the-night feeds to researching monthly milestones, we try to take on the world to give our baby the best. However, if you have a partner, it can be beneficial to have a conversation before baby arrives about sharing the load of household chores and responsibilities. This worksheet will help guide a discussion with your partner about how you will work together to manage the new parent load. The goal of openly communicating about and constantly refining these responsibilities is to help streamline decisions and prevent burnout and resentment.

DISCUSS EACH RESPONSIBILITY, THEN AGREE WHO SHOULD TAKE ON EACH TASK (ME or PARTNER). FOR TASKS YOU'LL SHARE, ADD CHECK MARK IN BOTH.

RESPONSIBILITY	M	P	RESPONSIBILITY	M	P
GROCERY SHOPPING			HOME MAINTENANCE		
MEAL PREPARATION			LANDSCAPING		
WASHING DISHES			VEHICLE MAINTENANCE		
TIDYING KITCHEN			FINANCES		
TAKING OUT GARBAGE			MAKING DR. APPTS.		
EMPTYING DISHWASHER			CHILDCARE		
VACUUMING			DRIVING CHILD TO/FROM ACTIVITIES		
LAUNDRY					
TIDYING LIVING SPACES			CHILDCARE COMMUNICATIONS		
CLEANING BATHROOM			SHOPPING FOR CHILD NECESSITIES		
MAKING BEDS					
DEEP CLEANING			MAINTAIN FAMILY CALENDAR		
SHOPPING FOR HOME ESSENTIALS			PET CARE		

Ways Your Partner

CAN HELP POSTPARTUM

Coming home with a new baby is a whirlwind. The constant cycle of feeding, diapers, and soothing, coupled with sleep deprivation, will push you to unthinkable limits. So many new parent responsibilities can feel like they're reserved for moms. Still, your partner can share the load during the fourth trimester in many ways beyond preparing bottles and changing diapers. Sometimes, our partners aren't sure how best to help. Other times, we're too overwhelmed to think about how best they can help. This list will help you think outside of the box regarding ways your partner can help you manage the new parent load.

AT THE HOSPITAL/ BIRTHING CENTER

- Advocate for your partner to the doctors and nurses.

  - If there are specific birth preferences, become familiar with them to ensure they are being met.
  - Ask how she's feeling. Ask how to help her pain best. For example, if breastfeeding is painful, ask if she can get additional support from a lactation consultant, a pump, or a nipple shield.

- Make sure enough food and water is available in the recovery room.
- Contact the pediatrician to say your baby was born and schedule the first appointment.
- Take notes when the doctor answers the **Questions to Ask the Doctor before Leaving the Hospital** (p. 141).

- If the doctor recommends any follow-up appointments, schedule them (e.g., tongue tie, hearing, etc.).
- Organize a folder so the informational paperwork is separate from the documents you need when you get home.
- If you haven't already, install the car seat.

AT HOME (RIGHT AWAY)

- If mom is breastfeeding, book a lactation consultant. Breastfeeding can be tricky. Lactation consultants are well-versed in the challenges and will offer various potential solutions.
- Apply for baby's birth certificate and baby's social security card.
- Learn how to sanitize pump parts/ bottles/pacifiers and how to safely prepare/store breast milk or formula.
- Make an outline of which bills are due when, and put the reminders on your phone to ensure they are paid on time. Consider setting some or all of your bills on auto-pay.

AT HOME (DAY-TO-DAY)

- Own certain house chores **from start to finish** (e.g., dishes, laundry, walking the dog, or cooking breakfast) so that it's not a conversation every time a particular chore needs to be done.
- Own at least one daily "baby" chore (e.g., the morning bottle, bath-time, an evening tummy time session, etc.) so that mom has a consistent time to look forward to every day.
- Place the online order for diapers, spare bottles, pump parts, and anything you think will make your life easier during the initial grind (read: paper plates and bowls, a robot vacuum, etc.)!
- Take baby out for a walk to give mom some alone time. Offer to take baby alone, but tell her she's welcome to join if she needs fresh air.
- Do the grocery shopping (or, even easier, submit the grocery delivery or pickup order).

NICU

- If your baby requires a NICU stay, take lots of photos during your visit and show them to mom when you get home.
- Ask the doctors questions and write down the answers so you can discuss them with mom when you get home.
- Learn how to store and transport breast milk safely.
- Once you've agreed on and with whom to share, help keep family and friends updated regarding the baby's condition.
- Find and join a support group as a couple.

Questions to Ask a Potential Doula

FOR YOUR LABOR SUPPORT TEAM

A doula is a professional birth coach or guide who can be hired to provide support both emotionally and physically, throughout your pregnancy, labor and delivery, and the postpartum period. Doulas **do not provide medical care** but are focused on helping you achieve a positive birth experience. Some studies have found that the benefits of working with a doula include shortened labor, decreased need for pain-relief medication, fewer operative deliveries, and increased maternal satisfaction post-labor (March of Dimes, 2022).

You can ask friends, family, or your OB/GYN for recommendations to find a doula. The Doula Organization of North America (DONA) is also an excellent resource for finding a doula near you. If you'd like a doula on your labor and delivery support team, these questions can help determine who fits your needs best.

NAME: _____ DATE: _____ / _____ / _____

TRAINING AND EXPERIENCE

Why did you decide to become a doula?

_____

_____

Are you formally trained as a doula? If so, which organization did you train with? For how long? Any advanced training?

_____

_____

Are you certified, or are you working toward certification?

_____

_____

When did you start practicing? How many births and what variety have you attended?

_____

_____

PHILOSOPHY AND APPROACH

How will you support me during labor? Which techniques do you use?

_____

_____

Do you bring anything specific to a birth?

_____

_____

How do you handle births that do not go "according to plan"? Are there any practices that you do not support (e.g., induction, epidural, cesarean)?

_____

_____

How will you support and include my partner during labor?

_____

What is your greatest strength? What do you find most challenging?

_____

_____

Do you assist with breastfeeding support? What experience and training do you have with breastfeeding?

_____

_____

Can you share a reference with whom I can speak?

_____

_____

What is your philosophy on hospital birth vs. birthing center vs. home birth?

_____

_____

What is your relationship like with hospital staff/other care providers? How do you handle a conflict between what I want and what a provider recommends?

_____

_____

LOGISTICS

Can I call you outside of our formal visits? Can I call anytime, or do you have specific working hours?

_____

_____

Are you available on my due date? If so, how many clients do you have around it?

_____

_____

When do you go on-call for me?

_____

_____

_____

What is the protocol if I go into labor before or after you're on-call?

_____

_____

How far into labor will you join me?

_____

How long do you stay after the birth?

_____

Do you have a backup doula or a network of backups? Is it possible to meet one? How did you choose them?

_____
_____
_____

Have you attended a birth where I intend to deliver (hospital, birthing center, at home)?

_____
_____

COST AND SERVICES

What is your full fee?

_____
_____
_____

What does your pricing include? How many visits do you make during pregnancy and postpartum?

_____
_____
_____

Are there any additional fees that may arise?

_____
_____

Do you require a deposit? If so, when is it due?

_____
_____

Which payment methods do you accept?

_____

Are there any circumstances where you offer a full or partial refund? If so, in what case (e.g., you and backup cannot attend birth, or I give birth before you arrive)?

_____

_____

_____

Do you have a formal contract to sign? Can I review a copy?

_____

_____

ADDITIONAL NOTES

_____

_____

_____

_____

_____

_____

_____

_____

_____

_____

_____

_____

_____

_____

_____

_____

Questions to Ask a Potential Daycare

GENERAL

Is this daycare licensed? Accredited? By whom?

_____

_____

How long has this daycare been operating?

_____

_____

Do you have any openings currently, or do I need to join a waitlist?

_____

_____

What is the cost? Are there any discounts?

_____

_____

What are your hours of operation? Do you offer part-time? If so, what is the part-time schedule?

_____

_____

What is your teacher/baby ratio?

_____

_____

What is the cost?

_____

_____

Which payment methods do you accept?

_____

_____

Will you change cloth diapers, or do we need to use disposable ones?

_____

_____

What is the policy if we are running late for pickup?

_____

_____

What is your sick-child policy?

_____

_____

Do you have any policies related to immunizations?

_____

_____

Will you ever take my baby off-site (e.g., walk to a park or a field trip)? If so, what stroller or vehicle would you use?

_____

_____

Can you share a reference?

_____

_____

_____

ENRICHMENT

What activities will you perform with my baby?

0-3 M

_____

_____

3-6M

_____

_____

6-9M

_____

_____

9-12M

_____

_____

What ages of other babies will mine be with?

_____

_____

_____

What temperatures do you take babies outside vs. staying in the classroom?

_____

_____

Will I know my child's daily activities, feedings, and naps?

_____

_____

_____

FEEDING

What protocols are in place for safely storing/serving breast milk?

_____

_____

Will I be informed of how much my baby ate during each feeding (i.e., # of ounces)?

_____

_____

Once my baby is ready for solids, will you help them do baby-led weaning, or is spoon-feeding required?

_____

_____

Do I have to send the solid food in with my baby, or are foods any provided?

_____

_____

How are allergies handled?

_____

_____

Are you a nut-free facility?

_____

EMPLOYEES

Does the staff have certifications or degrees?

_____

_____

What type of training have they had?

_____

Have all employees passed a background check?

_____

_____

What is the employee turnover rate?

_____

_____

How long have my baby's teachers been employed here?

_____

_____

What is the protocol in case of a medical emergency?

_____

_____

Do you have a nurse on site who can administer medicine or allergy treatments?

_____

SECURITY

Who can I designate to pick up my baby? What "steps" does someone have to follow to pick up my baby?

_____

_____

Do you have cameras at the entrance? In the rooms?

_____

What is your visitation policy for parents vs. others? Can I swing by at any point?

_____

_____

GERMS

What precautions are taken to help prevent the spread of germs?

_____

_____

How often do you sanitize the toys, surfaces, etc.?

_____

_____

What is the protocol if my baby becomes sick during the day?

_____

_____

_____

Will you inform us when other babies in the class are sick?

_____

_____

ADDITIONAL NOTES

_____

_____

_____

_____

_____

_____

_____

_____

Questions to Ask a Potential Babysitter

FOR BABIES 6 WEEKS TO 1 YEAR

GENERAL

How long have you been a caregiver?

_____

Do you have experience caring for a newborn? 3-6 months? 6-12 months?

_____

_____

What is your availability? Are you ever available on short notice? Are you flexible if I am running late?

_____

_____

Do you have a wage requirement?

_____

Do you have your own transportation?

_____

Do you have any allergies we need to know about (food, pets)?

_____

Are you willing to care for a pet/cook/clean/do light housework/[insert task] while caring for the baby?

_____

_____

HEALTH AND SAFETY

Do you understand safety standards for infant sleep?

_____

_____

Are you comfortable changing diapers? Handling a blowout?

_____

Have you bathed a baby? Are you comfortable keeping the bath safe?

_____

Have you prepared and sterilized a bottle of breastmilk? Formula?

_____

_____

Are you comfortable with baby-led weaning and spoon-feeding? Have you spoon-fed or supervised a baby eating before? Are you familiar with choking hazards?

_____

_____

How would you handle a difficult situation, like the baby crying uncontrollably? Are you comfortable taking action if my child is choking?

_____

_____

Do you have any formal safety or childcare certifications? CPR? First Aid?

_____

_____

Can you share a reference?

_____

_____

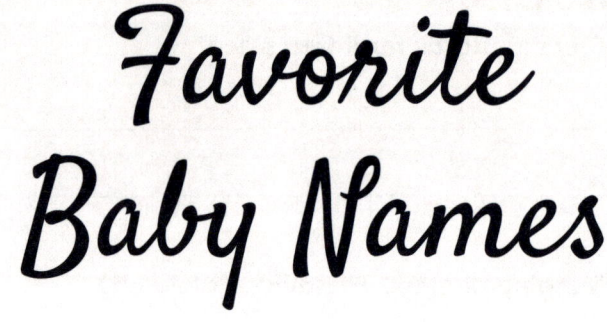

Favorite Baby Names

20 Week Ultrasound

DATE: _____

ADDITIONAL NOTES

_____

_____

_____

_____

_____

_____

_____

Third Trimester

WEEKS
28-40+

Third Trimester Checklist

You've made it to the third trimester—can you believe it?! Even though you may be unable to touch your toes, you're getting close to the finish line! You can do these things during the third trimester to prepare for baby's arrival.

GENERAL

☐ Continue taking a daily prenatal vitamin with folate or folic acid and drinking plenty of water.

☐ Set up the bassinet or crib in your bedroom.

*The AAP recommends that your baby share the **same room** (but not the same bed) as you for the first six months because it can reduce the risk of SIDS by as much as 50% (Moon & AAP, 2022).*

☐ Assemble gear you'll use in the first few months (stroller, swing, play gym for tummy time, bassinet or crib, etc.).

☐ Install the car seat around 34 weeks.

If you get into an accident while the car seat is installed, check with the manufacturer to see if you need to replace it. Your auto insurance may replace it for free, but it can take a few weeks.

☐ Pack your hospital bag around 36 weeks. Encourage your partner, if applicable, to pack a bag as well.

☐ Pack your baby's diaper bag to bring to the hospital.

☐ Locate the documents the hospital requires for labor day. Put any documents you don't need daily in a folder in your hospital bag.

☐ If you plan to breastfeed, check with your insurance provider about getting your free pump around 28 weeks.

☐ Sanitize pump parts and assemble them to ensure that they turn on.

☐ Purchase anything left on your registry that you want before baby's arrival.

☐ If you had a baby shower, send thank you notes.

☐ Pamper yourself while you have the time and energy (haircut, manicure, etc.).

☐ Stock up on everyday essentials (toiletries, household supplies, etc.).

☐ Consider taking a CPR course in person or online.

☐ Decide who will care for your pets once you go into labor. Share a house key with the pet sitter if applicable.

Ensure your pets are up-to-date on shots if they will be boarded.

☐ Learn about newborn basics:
  - safe sleep
  - sleep cues
  - hunger cues
  - tummy time
  - sample feeding/sleeping "schedules"
  - when to call the pediatrician or 911 about a health concern
  - proper car seat installation + buckling

☐ Test smoke and carbon monoxide detectors and replace batteries.

DOCTOR, DOCTOR

☐ If your doctor recommends, consider a chiropractor or prenatal massage to alleviate any back pain you may be experiencing.

☐ If your doctor approves, do pelvic floor exercises to strengthen it.

☐ Ask your doctor about counting kicks, and start keeping track of your baby's activity.

☐ Learn about contractions (Braxton Hicks vs. true labor contractions) and how to time them.

☐ Ask your doctor when you should go to the hospital for labor and if you can eat/drink before coming in.

☐ Attend a hospital tour, ask questions (p. 80), and register for delivery, if applicable.

☐ Finalize your **Birth Preferences Worksheet** (p. 95). Print a few copies to put in your hospital bag.

☐ Schedule your delivery if it is planned (induction, C-Section, etc.).

☐ Interview and select a pediatrician who accepts your insurance (p. 90).

Questions to Ask on a Hospital Tour

BEFORE THE BIG DAY

Hospital tours are often offered to prospective parents in person or virtually. Attending a tour between 30 and 34 weeks should give you enough time to prepare without forgetting where to go for check-in! If you have the opportunity to choose between more than one hospital, getting answers to these questions may help you decide where you prefer to deliver. Even if there is only one option in your area, knowing what to expect will help you approach the big day more confidently.

HOSPITAL NAME: _____

HOSPITAL ADDRESS: _____

_____

PRE-LABOR

Do you offer pregnancy, labor and delivery, postpartum care, or baby care courses? If so, are they online or in-person, and how can I sign up? Is there a cost?

_____

_____

Is there any pre-admission paperwork I need to complete? If so, should I send it beforehand via email or bring it with me the day of?

_____

_____

CHECKING IN DAY OF

Where should I go when I arrive? Is it the same location for overnight, a scheduled induction, or a scheduled Cesarean?

_____

_____

What is the protocol for parking, and how much does it cost? Do you offer valet?

_____

_____

Which form(s) of identification are required to bring the day of? My partner?

_____

_____

Will OB/GYN send a copy of my chart, or do I need to bring a copy?

_____

Do you require me to bring anything specific for labor?

_____

_____

ACCOMMODATIONS

Are the labor and delivery rooms private or shared? Is there a private bathroom?

_____

Are there different types of labor and delivery rooms (e.g., bathtub vs. shower)? Do fees differ based on room type?

_____

_____

May I request a specific labor and delivery room type to accommodate my birth preferences (e.g., bathtub)?

_____

_____

What's the protocol if the labor and delivery floor is full? How often does this happen?

_____

_____

_____

Are the recovery rooms separate from the labor and delivery rooms? If so, are they private with a private restroom? When will we move?

_____

_____

What is the average length of stay for a vaginal delivery? Cesarean?

_____

_____

Which postpartum recovery items do you provide (e.g., pads, frozen pads, peri bottle, sitz bath, heating pad, hemorrhoid pillow, non-slip socks, etc.)?

_____

_____

Can my partner or support person stay overnight? If so, is there a place for them to sleep?

_____

Can I bring pillows, blankets, towels, and toiletries from home to be more comfortable during my stay?

_____

_____

Do you provide food or drinks during labor, or can I bring my own? What can I have?

_____

_____

Can I bring my own food and drinks for recovery? Will I have access to a refrigerator?

_____

_____

Are meal costs included for me (or my partner)? Is food available 24/7? Can the kitchen accommodate diet restrictions?

_____

LABOR + DELIVERY

How many patients are typically assigned to each nurse (i.e., nurse-to-patient ratio)?

_____

_____

Can I labor at my own speed, or is there a dilation time limit?

_____

_____

Which method is typically used for fetal monitoring? Periodic (auscultation using a fetoscope or Doppler) vs. continuous electronic (internal or external)?

_____

_____

_____

What birthing equipment do you offer? _____

_____

Do you offer saline locks? _____

_____

Is this a teaching hospital? Will medical residents/interns/students attend my labor and birth? Can I request privacy if I am uncomfortable with them attending?

_____

_____

_____

If preferred, can I:

push in a position other than on my back? ☐ **Yes** ☐ **No**

wear a labor and delivery gown from home? ☐ **Yes** ☐ **No**

deliver in the shower or bathtub? ☐ **Yes** ☐ **No**

have photos and videos taken? ☐ **Yes** ☐ **No**

CESAREAN BIRTH (C-SECTION)

What pain relief medications are available prior to the operation?

_____

_____

If preferred, can I watch (mirror, lowered, or clear drape)?

_____

_____

Can my partner or support person attend?

_____

Can I hold my baby right away (skin-to-skin)? Nurse?

_____

_____

If you need to take my baby elsewhere, can my partner accompany them?

_____

_____

Which pain relief options are typically offered post-operation?

_____

_____

Can we take photos or videos? _____

_____

MEDICATION + PAIN MANAGEMENT

What medication options are available for pain management (nitrous oxide, epidural)?

_____

_____

Is epidural anesthesia available 24/7? How long is the typical wait between requesting an epidural and receiving it?

_____

_____

Is anything required beforehand to receive an epidural (class, signed form, etc.)?

_____

Can I meet with an anesthesiologist before or during labor if I have other questions about epidurals?

_____

_____

DOULA + MIDWIFE

Does my doula or midwife need to bring specific identification or paperwork?

_____

_____

Can my doula or midwife attend labor? Cesarean birth?

_____

_____

Are there doulas or midwives on staff?

_____

BABY CARE

If preferred, can I:

do skin-to-skin before baby's exams?   ☐ **Yes**   ☐ **No**

delay cord clamping?   ☐ **Yes**   ☐ **No**

bank or donate my baby's cord blood?   ☐ **Yes**   ☐ **No**

What is the rooming-in vs. nursery policy?

_____

_____

Do you have an on-site pediatrician who will examine my baby, or should my pediatrician come to the hospital to examine the baby? If it is my pediatrician, who notifies them that the baby was born and needs to be examined?

_____

_____

_____

Do you offer 24/7 lactation consultation and support? Are consultants certified?

_____

_____

Will I have access to an industrial-grade breast pump if needed?

_____

_____

What is the protocol for supplementing with formula?

_____

_____

If I plan to formula-feed from the start, who should I tell? Do you supply formula or bottles, or do I need to bring them? Where can I wash bottles?

_____

_____

_____

What is your policy for pacifiers? _____

_____

_____

Do you supply swaddles, diapers, and wipes? Anything else?

_____

_____

What infant security protocols do you have (e.g., I.D. bands, electronic monitors, alarms, etc.)?

_____

_____

Who performs a circumcision, if preferred? Where is it performed?

_____

_____

Do you offer any:

baby-care/safety classes before I leave? ☐ **Yes** ☐ **No**

newborn photography sessions? ☐ **Yes** ☐ **No**

postpartum resources*? ☐ **Yes** ☐ **No**

_____

_____

*e.g., breastfeeding support groups, perinatal mood disorder support, etc

VISITORS

How many support people can I have with me during labor? What form(s) of identification should they bring? Where should they enter?

_____

_____

How many people can visit during recovery? What form(s) of identification should they bring? Where should they enter?

_____

What are the visiting hours? Are they different for labor vs. recovery?

_____

Can children visit? Is there an age restriction?

_____

_____

Is the maternity unit locked? What other safety protocols do you have to ensure we are kept safe?

_____

_____

NEONATAL INTENSIVE CARE UNIT

Do you have a NICU on-site? If so, which level is your NICU (I, II, III, IV)? Specialties?

_____

_____

Which floor of the hospital is it on? How far is the NICU from the recovery rooms?

_____

_____

If my baby needs additional care outside of this hospital, where will they be transferred?

_____

_____

What is the NICU visitor policy?
What are the NICU visiting hours?

_____

_____

_____

_____

_____

_____

ADDITIONAL CONSIDERATIONS

What is the hospital's rate for:

Cesarean birth: _____

Induction: _____

Augmentation during labor: _____

Epidural: _____

Episiotomy: _____

Vacuum/forceps: _____

Vaginal birth after cesarean (VBAC): _____

Maternal mortality: _____

Maternal mortality (people of color): _____

Infant mortality: _____

Average cost for vaginal birth: _____

Average cost for cesarean: _____

ADDITIONAL NOTES

_____

_____

_____

_____

_____

_____

_____

_____

_____

_____

Questions to Ask a Potential Pediatrician

BEFORE BABY ARRIVES

PEDIATRICIAN OFFICE NAME + PHONE NUMBER: _____
_____

PEDIATRICIAN NAME(S): _____
_____

Can I meet the doctor(s) and see the office before baby arrives?
_____

Do you take my insurance? _____

Which hospital are you affiliated with? _____
_____

How long have you been practicing? Are you board-certified? Specialties?
_____
_____
_____

Do you have a specific philosophy on breastfeeding, formula feeding, circumcision, sleep training, vaccines, potty training, and alternative medicine? If so, do you follow specific practices?
_____
_____
_____

If my baby ends up needing pediatric services immediately after birth, can and will you come to the hospital or center where I deliver?

_____

_____

_____

What happens if my baby needs to see a specialist for any reason?

_____

_____

If my baby becomes sick, do you offer same-day appointments?

_____

_____

_____

Can I contact the doctor when the office is closed (e.g., evenings, weekends, etc.)?

_____

_____

What's your policy on antibiotics? Vaccines?

_____

_____

Where will we go for blood work?

_____

_____

Can my partner attend the appointments?

_____

_____

_____

What to Pack in Your Hospital Bag

FOR CHILDBIRTH

Plan to have your hospital bag packed by 36 weeks. For items you can't pack quite yet (e.g., Driver's License, snacks, etc.), make sure they are easily accessible for go-time! Keep in mind that the hospital typically provides postpartum recovery and baby essentials (e.g., pads, peri bottle, newborn diapers, diaper rash ointment, etc.).

FOR MOM (LABOR AND DELIVERY)

- ☐ Driver's License or Government ID
- ☐ Insurance card
- ☐ Hospital forms (if applicable)
- ☐ Birth Preferences (2-3 copies)
- ☐ Folder for paperwork
- ☐ Pen
- ☐ Small notebook
- ☐ Water bottle
- ☐ Headphones
- ☐ Snacks (hospital permitting)

_____

_____

IF PREFERRED, FOR EXTRA COMFORT

- ☐ Hospital gown alternative (1-2)
- ☐ Comfortable clothes (oversized t-shirt, shorts, pajamas, robe) Typically, you can wear your own clothes postpartum if preferred. Your room may be hot or cold, so plan for either.

_____

_____

_____

FOR MOM (POSTPARTUM)

- ☐ Large, comfortable underwear
- ☐ Simple makeup bag (foundation, eyeliner, lip balm/color for photos)
- ☐ Prenatal vitamins
- ☐ Socks with grips

_____

_____

If planning to nurse or pump:

- ☐ Lanolin nipple cream
- ☐ Nursing bras
- ☐ Nursing-friendly shirts
- ☐ Silver nipple covers
- ☐ Nursing pads

_____

_____

FOR THE PARENT(S)

- [ ] Shampoo/conditioner/soap
- [ ] Toothbrush/toothpaste
- [ ] Deodorant
- [ ] Face wash/wipes
- [ ] Lotion
- [ ] Extra hair ties
- [ ] Glasses/contacts
- [ ] Prescribed medication (if applicable)
- [ ] Shower sandals/flip-flops
- [ ] Clothes for 2-3 days
- [ ] Phone charger and long cord
- [ ] Clothes for going home
- [ ] Snacks
- [ ] Cash (vending, valet tips)

_____

_____

_____

_____

IF PREFERRED, FOR EXTRA COMFORT

- [ ] Towels/washcloths
- [ ] Pillow (non-white pillowcase)
- [ ] Blanket
- [ ] Laptop/tablet
- [ ] Earplugs/eye mask

_____

_____

_____

_____

FOR BABY

- [ ] Car seat
- [ ] Diaper bag
- [ ] Outfits (preemie, newborn or 0-3M)
- [ ] Hat/beanie
- [ ] Socks
- [ ] Mittens
- [ ] Baby comb/brush
- [ ] Baby lotion
- [ ] Pacifier(s)
- [ ] Swaddle blanket
- [ ] Burp cloths
- [ ] Pediatrician contact information
- [ ] Hospital photoshoot items (e.g., special swaddle blanket, name sign, sentimental items, etc.)

_____

_____

_____

If planning to pump or formula feed, ask the hospital if you should bring:

- [ ] Breast pump
- [ ] Formula
- [ ] Bottles
- [ ] Cleaning supplies (dish soap, sponge, etc.)

FOR PET SITTING

- [ ] Food (3-4 days)
- [ ] Bed
- [ ] Bowl(s)
- [ ] Treats
- [ ] Toys
- [ ] Medication (if applicable)

_____

_____

Consider packing a **"definitely bring in"** bag and a **"might use"** bag to leave in the car.

You won't be burdened with too much to carry in or out, but you'll still have easy access to extras you might use.

Essential Documents for the Hospital

ON LABOR DAY

Now that your hospital bag is packed with cute little onesies and the biggest postpartum underwear you can find, it's time to start a folder with the important **documents to bring with you to the hospital** on labor day.

PREPARE BEFOREHAND :

- [ ] **Health Insurance Card:** If you don't have a physical copy, check your provider's website to request one or print/take a screenshot of the digital card.
- [ ] **Pediatrician Information:** Write down their name, phone number, and office name.
- [ ] **Medications:** Create a list of the over-the-counter and prescription medications you take.
- [ ] **Birth Preferences:** Print more than one copy to give to your doctor, nurses, and your support person.
- [ ] **Hospital Admissions Paperwork:** Remember, some hospitals require the paperwork to be submitted a few weeks before your due date.
- [ ] **Social Security Number:** Memorize it or write it down. If applicable, ask your partner to do so as well.
- [ ] **Marriage Certificate:** If applicable, it doesn't hurt to put a copy of your marriage certificate in your folder, especially if your last name differs from your partner's.
- [ ] **Prenatal Medical Records:** If your pregnancy has had any complications or you live far from the hospital, including these in your folder is a good idea.
- [ ] **Cord Blood Paperwork/Kit:** If you're planning to donate or bank baby's cord blood, bring the information.
- [ ] **Paper and Pen:** Bring a few loose pieces of paper or a notebook and a pen to take notes.

DAY OF:

- [ ] **Identification:** Driver's license, passport, or other government-provided form of identification
- [ ] **Partner's Identification:** Driver's license, passport, or other government-provided form of identification
- [ ] **Health Insurance Card:** Double-check that you packed a physical or digital copy.

Birth Preferences

FULL NAME: _____ DOCTOR/MIDWIFE: _____

LABOR COMPANION: _____ DUE DATE: _____

About Me

- ☐ Gestational diabetes
- ☐ Group B strep positive
- ☐ Herpes +
- ☐ Rh-negative

_____

_____

Delivery Preferences

- ☐ Push myself
- ☐ Be coached to push
- ☐ Use a variety of positions to push
- ☐ No forceps or vacuum, if possible
- ☐ Natural tearing preferred over an episiotomy

_____

Labor Preferences

- ☐ Dimmed lighting
- ☐ Saline lock if IV is needed
- ☐ Wireless monitoring in early labor

_____

_____

_____

Baby Care Preferences

- ☐ Delayed cord clamping
- ☐ Partner to cut cord
- ☐ Breastfeed immediately
- ☐ Feed with formula
- ☐ Circumcision

_____

_____

Pain Relief/Medication

- ☐ No medication desired.
- ☐ Please do not offer. I will ask.
- ☐ Please offer as soon as available.
- ☐ Epidural
- ☐ I have not decided.

_____

In Case of a Cesarean Birth

- ☐ Labor partner accompany to OR.
- ☐ If anesthesia, I prefer an epidural.
- ☐ If anesthesia, I prefer a spinal.
- ☐ I prefer to see the birth.
- ☐ I prefer to hold my baby in the OR.

_____

Breastfeeding Essentials + Tips

WHAT TO HAVE AT HOME IF YOU PLAN TO BREASTFEED

FOR MOM

- Lanolin nipple cream or balm
- Nursing bras (options for daytime use and others comfortable enough for sleep)
- Breast pads (disposable, reusable)
- Nursing-friendly shirts
- Nursing tank tops or camisoles
- Nursing pillow
- Hot/cold breast therapy gel packs
- Silver nursing cups
- Nursing cover or scarf

FOR PUMPING, STORING, AND FEEDING YOUR BABY PUMPED BREAST MILK

- Silicone Manual Breast Pump or Milk Catcher (more than one if you use often)
- Double electric breast pump or hands-free pump (if you plan to pump frequently) and spare parts
- Hands-free pumping bra (if the pump is not wireless)
- Breast milk storage containers (bags, bottles, or glass containers designed specifically for breast milk)
- Colored sticker labels or colored permanent markers (color-code bags by month to easily identify in the freezer)
- Bottles
- Dishwasher basket
- Bottle/pump parts sterilizer
- Cooler/cold packs to transport stored milk

FOR ADDITIONAL SUPPORT

- A prenatal breastfeeding class
- Support from a lactation professional

  - Ask your healthcare provider or search the **U.S. Lactation Consultant Association** to find an international board-certified lactation consultant, or IBCLC, in your area.

- Breast shells/nipple shields or other products for inverted or flat nipples
- A notepad or a breastfeeding app to track feedings

TIPS FOR BREASTFEEDING

- **Prepare:** Learn about breastfeeding before baby's arrival to better understand:

  - Latching
  - Preventing and caring for soreness in nipples or breasts
  - Milk supply and what you can do to help boost supply or find relief for engorgement
  - How often to feed your baby during the first days/weeks and as baby grows
  - Common breastfeeding issues
  - How to store and prepare breast milk if you plan to pump

- **Get comfortable:** To prevent or ease back and neck pain, practice various breastfeeding positions and find calming spots in your home for you and your baby. For some moms, sitting in a reclining chair or glider and using a pregnancy or nursing pillow helps provide additional support and comfort. A certified lactation consultant can suggest different breastfeeding positions.
- **Get organized:** Create a breastfeeding or pumping station with a water bottle, healthy snacks, hand sanitizer, tissues, your breast pump, burp cloths, diapers, wet wipes, and extra outfits for baby so you have everything within reach when you sit down to feed or pump.

TIPS FOR BOTTLE FEEDING YOUR BABY BREAST MILK

- You do not need to serve breast milk warm. If baby gets used to room temperature or cold breast milk, you can serve your baby a bottle of freshly-expressed or refrigerated breast milk.
- Color code frozen breast milk bags by month with colored stickers or permanent markers so you can easily identify them in the freezer.
- Try a few different bottle types to see what you and your baby prefer.
- Once you've chosen a bottle brand you like, buy some of each size. You can also purchase different-sized nipples, but the larger bottles typically come with larger nipples you can also use on the smaller bottles once ready.
- Get enough bottles to avoid having to wash them more than once per day. Even easier, put them in the dishwasher and run the dishwasher each night.
- Research FDA guidelines for cleaning a breast pump.

ONLINE BREASTFEEDING RESOURCES, CLASSES, AND SUPPORT:

- Breastfeeding 101 by Milky Mama
- La Leche League
- Lactation Link (Courses and e-Consults)
- Milkology (Freebie Library and Online Courses)
- Medela's Breastfeeding University
- Stanford Medicine: Getting Started with Breastfeeding

Breast Milk Storage

+ HOW TO THAW

BREAST MILK STORAGE

The CDC recommends the following for storing and thawing breast milk (2022a):

- Always write the date and time on the breast milk storage bag.
- To freeze breast milk, use breast milk storage bags and **lay them flat** in the freezer.
- Milk can be stored in an insulated cooler bag with frozen ice packs for up to 24 hours when traveling.
- Store milk in the back of the freezer or refrigerator, not by the door.

THAWING FROZEN BREAST MILK

- Thaw the oldest milk first.
- Place frozen breast milk in lukewarm tap water in a clean, empty container.
- Place frozen breast milk in the refrigerator overnight.
- Use breast milk within 24 hours of thawing in the refrigerator (from the time it is completely thawed, not the time you took it out of the freezer).
- **Do not** put it in boiling water, the microwave, or on the stovetop.
- **Do not refreeze** after thawing.

TYPE OF BREAST MILK	COUNTERTOP 77°F (25°C) or Colder	REFRIGERATOR 40°F (<4°C)	FREEZER 0°F (-18°C) or Colder
Freshly expressed or pumped	Up to 4 hours	Up to 4 days	Within 6 months (ideal) Up to 12 months (acceptable)
Thawed, previously frozen	1-2 hours	Up to 1 day (24 hours)	*Never refreeze human milk after it has been thawed*

If your baby does not finish the bottle of breast milk, the leftovers should be used within 2 hours or thrown away.

Formula Feeding Essentials + Tips

WHAT TO HAVE AT HOME IF YOU PLAN TO FEED FORMULA

WHAT'S NEEDED?

- Formula (talk to your pediatrician about which brand to use)
- Bottles

WHAT'S NICE TO HAVE?

- Bottle drying rack
- Dishwasher basket

TIPS + TRICKS FOR FORMULA FEEDING

- You don't need to serve formula warm. If your baby gets used to room-temperature formula, it will save you a step every time!
- Try a few different bottle types to see what you and your baby prefer.
- Get enough bottles to avoid having to wash them more than once per day. Even easier, put them in the dishwasher and run the dishwasher each night.
- When planning to be away from home, add powdered formula to a divided formula dispenser or small plastic containers. Then, add the correct amounts of water to the number of bottles you think you'll use, and put them in a wet/dry bag (designed for cloth diapers). Finally, when your baby is hungry, you can simply add the formula to the pre-measured water in the bottles.

RECOMMENDATIONS FROM THE CDC (2023A):

- Before making a bottle for your baby, **wash your hands** and sanitize the area where you will prepare it.
- **Never use a microwave to warm a bottle**. Instead, place it under warm running water or use a bottle warmer. Test the temperature on your hand before serving.
- Always **measure the water first** and then add the formula.
- Use the bottle **within 2 hours of preparation**.
- Use the bottle **within 1 hour** from when you **started feeding** your baby.
- If you are not feeding within 2 hours of preparation, immediately store it in the refrigerator and use it within 24 hours.
- If your baby does not finish the bottle of formula, the **leftover formula should be used within 1 hour or thrown away**.
- Check your formula's label for storage requirements. Typically, powder formula should be stored in a cool, dry place in your home (but not the refrigerator) and used within 1 month of opening.

Safe Sleep 101

While you will cherish every moment you and your baby sleep very soon, learning how best to keep your baby safe during those precious moments is important. Research from the American Academy of Pediatrics (2022a) has found that "sleep-related death can occur when an infant with an intrinsic vulnerability to SIDS (Sudden Infant Death Syndrome) is placed in an unsafe sleep environment." While the possibility of SIDS can feel scary and overwhelming, it is important to keep in mind a mantra we often remind ourselves as new mothers: "**I can only control what I can control**." So, while you cannot control whether your baby is more vulnerable to SIDS, you can control your baby's sleep environment and ensure it is as safe as possible.

The American Academy of Pediatrics (2022a) provides the following recommendations to reduce the risk of sleep-related deaths in infants:

- baby should sleep on a **firm, flat, noninclined surface** that "meets existing federal safety standards for cribs, bassinets, play yards, and bedside sleepers."
- always place your baby into their bassinet or crib **on their back**.

  - stop swaddling baby once they show signs of trying to roll onto their stomach (usually around three or four months but can be earlier).

- do not put any soft toys, pillows, blankets, or other bedding in the crib or bassinet.
- do not use devices intended for sitting for routine sleep, especially if baby is less than four months old (e.g., car seat, stroller, swing, infant carriers/slings).

- breastfeed, if possible.

  - "While any human milk feeding is more protective than none, 2 months of feeding at least partial human milk feeding has been demonstrated to significantly lower the risk of sleep-related deaths."

- sleep in the same room as baby, but not the same bed, for the first six months.
- avoid nicotine, alcohol, marijuana, opioids, and illicit drug exposure.
- immunize your baby according to the standard schedule.
- provide baby with a pacifier when going to sleep.

_____
_____
_____
_____

- build up your baby's neck strength with supervised tummy time when awake.

  - Start with short periods of time once you're home from the hospital, and increase slowly to about 15-30 minutes per day by seven weeks of age

- do not use weighted swaddles, objects, or clothing.
- do not use home cardiorespiratory monitors as a strategy to reduce the risk of SIDS.

CO-SLEEPING/BEDSHARING

The AAP (2022a) is very adamant that sharing the same bed as a baby "significantly raises the risk of a baby's injury or death."

- Specifically, the AAP has found that the "risks of sleeping on the same surface with someone else also increase 5-10 times when an infant is under four months of age; is sharing the surface with someone other than a parent; or is a pre-term or low-birthweight, regardless of other factors."
- The AAP also points out that "the risks of sleep-related infant deaths are up to 67 times higher when sleeping with someone on a couch or soft armchair or cushion."

It is also important to acknowledge that, even given the risks, some parents choose to share the same bed as their baby, even if they did not initially plan to do so. La Leche League International (Wiessinger et al., 2018) suggests that a breastfeeding mother follow these guidelines if they share the same bed as their baby:

- Do not smoke in the home or outside.
- Do not use drugs, alcohol, or any medication that causes drowsiness.
- Breastfeed day and night.
- Baby should be healthy and full-term.
- Baby should sleep on their back with the face-up.
- Baby should be in light clothing and not swaddled to avoid overheating.
- Baby should sleep on a firm mattress:

  - without any extra pillows, toys, tight or heavy covers.
  - without any strings or cords.
  - with gaps firmly filled (rolled towels or rolled baby blankets).

As a reminder, **bed-sharing is not recommended by the American Academy of Pediatrics** (2022a).

If you find yourself struggling with your baby's sleep, talk to your baby's pediatrician. Getting enough sleep is critical for your mental health and well-being. The pediatrician will partner with you and develop strategies for keeping your baby safe while sleeping.

Baby Caretaking Rules

When we become parents, we are thrust into a whirlwind of endless decision-making around what is in the best interest of our new baby. Discussing and agreeing upon some general caretaking "rules" with your partner or baby's future caregiver before their arrival may help you work through potential differences in parenting styles. It will also lay the foundation for future sleep-deprived caretaking decisions that will arise or need refining.

This worksheet will help guide a discussion with your partner or baby's future caregiver about which caretaking decisions you agree to uphold. These preemptive and open conversations will help streamline decisions and ensure you are on the same page and the same team when caring for your baby.

The following are some examples to help get the conversation started. Write your baby's caretaking rules on the next page.

1   We will buckle baby in the car seat every time they're in the car.

2   We will not feed baby honey or anything flavored with honey before the first birthday.

3   We will not fall asleep on the couch or in a chair while holding baby.

4   We will always stay within arm's reach of baby on tall surfaces (bed, changing table) or in water (bathtub, pool).

5   We will not let baby nap in the car seat outside of the car.

Baby's Caretaking Rules

Kick Counter

FETAL MOVEMENT LOG

Before using this worksheet, talk to your provider about fetal movement counting and when to call with a concern.

The American Congress of Obstetricians and Gynecologists (ACOG) recommends you **time how long it takes you to feel 10 kicks, flutters, swishes, or rolls, ideally within 2 hours or less** (American Pregnancy Association, 2021). Track your baby's movement around the same time each day. Many babies are most active in the evening after a meal. Your provider may recommend you call them if you don't feel 10 movements within 2 hours or if the time it takes to feel 10 movements is longer than usual for your baby.

DATE MM/DD	START HH:MM	BABY MOVEMENTS (KICKS, ROLLS, JABS)	END HH:MM	DURATION ~<2 HOURS

Kick Counter

FETAL MOVEMENT LOG

DATE MM/DD	START HH:MM	BABY MOVEMENTS (KICKS, ROLLS, JABS)	END HH:MM	DURATION ~<2 HOURS
		□□□□□□□□□		
		□□□□□□□□□		
		□□□□□□□□□		
		□□□□□□□□□		
		□□□□□□□□□		
		□□□□□□□□□		
		□□□□□□□□□		
		□□□□□□□□□		
		□□□□□□□□□		
		□□□□□□□□□		
		□□□□□□□□□		
		□□□□□□□□□		
		□□□□□□□□□		

Kick Counter

FETAL MOVEMENT LOG

Before using this worksheet, talk to your provider about fetal movement counting and when to call with a concern.

DATE MM/DD	START HH:MM	BABY MOVEMENTS (KICKS, ROLLS, JABS)	END HH:MM	DURATION ~<2 HOURS
		☐ ☐ ☐ ☐ ☐ ☐ ☐ ☐ ☐ ☐		
		☐ ☐ ☐ ☐ ☐ ☐ ☐ ☐ ☐ ☐		
		☐ ☐ ☐ ☐ ☐ ☐ ☐ ☐ ☐ ☐		
		☐ ☐ ☐ ☐ ☐ ☐ ☐ ☐ ☐ ☐		
		☐ ☐ ☐ ☐ ☐ ☐ ☐ ☐ ☐ ☐		
		☐ ☐ ☐ ☐ ☐ ☐ ☐ ☐ ☐ ☐		
		☐ ☐ ☐ ☐ ☐ ☐ ☐ ☐ ☐ ☐		
		☐ ☐ ☐ ☐ ☐ ☐ ☐ ☐ ☐ ☐		
		☐ ☐ ☐ ☐ ☐ ☐ ☐ ☐ ☐ ☐		
		☐ ☐ ☐ ☐ ☐ ☐ ☐ ☐ ☐ ☐		
		☐ ☐ ☐ ☐ ☐ ☐ ☐ ☐ ☐ ☐		
		☐ ☐ ☐ ☐ ☐ ☐ ☐ ☐ ☐ ☐		
		☐ ☐ ☐ ☐ ☐ ☐ ☐ ☐ ☐ ☐		
		☐ ☐ ☐ ☐ ☐ ☐ ☐ ☐ ☐ ☐		

THIRD TRIMESTER

Kick Counter

FETAL MOVEMENT LOG

DATE MM/DD	START HH:MM	BABY MOVEMENTS (KICKS, ROLLS, JABS)	END HH:MM	DURATION ~<2 HOURS
		▢▢▢▢▢▢▢▢▢▢		
		▢▢▢▢▢▢▢▢▢▢		
		▢▢▢▢▢▢▢▢▢▢		
		▢▢▢▢▢▢▢▢▢▢		
		▢▢▢▢▢▢▢▢▢▢		
		▢▢▢▢▢▢▢▢▢▢		
		▢▢▢▢▢▢▢▢▢▢		
		▢▢▢▢▢▢▢▢▢▢		
		▢▢▢▢▢▢▢▢▢▢		
		▢▢▢▢▢▢▢▢▢▢		
		▢▢▢▢▢▢▢▢▢▢		
		▢▢▢▢▢▢▢▢▢▢		
		▢▢▢▢▢▢▢▢▢▢		
		▢▢▢▢▢▢▢▢▢▢		

Kick Counter

FETAL MOVEMENT LOG

Before using this worksheet, talk to your provider about fetal movement counting and when to call with a concern.

DATE MM/DD	START HH:MM	BABY MOVEMENTS (KICKS, ROLLS, JABS)	END HH:MM	DURATION ~<2 HOURS

Kick Counter

FETAL MOVEMENT LOG

DATE MM/DD	START HH:MM	BABY MOVEMENTS (KICKS, ROLLS, JABS)	END HH:MM	DURATION ~<2 HOURS

Kick Counter

FETAL MOVEMENT LOG

Before using this worksheet, talk to your provider about fetal movement counting and when to call with a concern.

DATE MM/DD	START HH:MM	BABY MOVEMENTS (KICKS, ROLLS, JABS)	END HH:MM	DURATION ~<2 HOURS

Baby Registry Gift Log

GIFT FROM	DESCRIPTION	THANK YOU SENT?
		☐
		☐
		☐
		☐
		☐
		☐
		☐
		☐
		☐
		☐
		☐

Baby Registry Gift Log

GIFT FROM	DESCRIPTION	THANK YOU SENT?
		☐
		☐
		☐
		☐
		☐
		☐
		☐
		☐
		☐
		☐
		☐

Baby Registry Gift Log

GIFT FROM	DESCRIPTION	THANK YOU SENT?
		☐
		☐
		☐
		☐
		☐
		☐
		☐
		☐
		☐
		☐
		☐

Final Preparations

What to Stock Up On Before Baby Arrives

Reminder: Always consult with your doctor before taking medication or giving medication to your baby.

LIST OF ESSENTIALS TO HAVE AT HOME

BATHROOM/MEDICINE CABINET

- [ ] Toilet paper
- [ ] Hand soap
- [ ] Shampoo/conditioner/soap
- [ ] Toothpaste
- [ ] Stool softener
- [ ] Maximum absorbency pads
- [ ] Pain relievers (consult your doctor)
- [ ] Prenatal vitamins

KITCHEN

- [ ] Dishwasher detergent
- [ ] Paper towels
- [ ] Paper plates
- [ ] Hand soap
- [ ] Baby dish soap
- [ ] Regular dish soap
- [ ] Disinfectant wipes/spray
- [ ] Frozen meals
- [ ] Coffee/tea

LAUNDRY

- [ ] Fragrance-free laundry detergent
- [ ] Fragrance-free dryer sheets
- [ ] Stain remover

MISCELLANEOUS

- [ ] Hand sanitizer
- [ ] Pet food/supplies

VAGINAL DELIVERY RECOVERY

- [ ] Large, comfortable underwear
- [ ] Witch hazel pads
- [ ] Lidocaine spray

C-SECTION RECOVERY

- [ ] Large, comfortable, high-waisted, or compression underwear
- [ ] Silicone scar sheets
- [ ] Nursing pillow
- [ ] Abdominal binder

IF PLANNING TO BREASTFEED

- [ ] Lanolin cream
- [ ] Nursing bra
- [ ] Nursing pads

BABY

- [ ] Diapers (newborn + size 1)
- [ ] Sensitive wipes
- [ ] Petroleum jelly (if planning to have baby circumcised)
- [ ] Alcohol pads to clean around umbilical cord
- [ ] Gas drops
- [ ] Vitamin D drops (if planning to breastfeed)
- [ ] Formula (if planning to formula feed, or as a backup in case pediatrician recommends supplementing)

Ways to Take Care of Yourself

AS A NEW MOM

Keep in mind that **your mental health and well-being are important** and worth prioritizing. In the early days, it is easy to be swept up by baby's unending needs. However, just as flight attendants remind us on airplanes, you need to put your own oxygen mask on before helping others. Consider which, if any, of these suggestions resonate with you so that when you're in the thick of it, you will remember to keep your well-being top of mind.

SLEEP

Consider **creating a sleep schedule with your partner**, if applicable, that allows you both to have an uninterrupted sleep.

- For example, one person can sleep from 8 P.M. to 2 A.M. and the other from 2 A.M. to 8 A.M. with a brief wake-up to pump or breastfeed, if applicable.
- If you are solely handling night feedings/wakings for any reason, talk to your partner about identifying 2-3 hours each night when you can sleep uninterruptedly, knowing the baby is in your partner's care. This time can be in the evening (for example, after baby's evening feeding until 10 or 11 P.M.) or in the early morning (for example, starting after a 3 or 4 A.M. feeding until your baby needs to eat again or your partner needs you to take the baby). Even a short, uninterrupted stretch will go a long way in the first few weeks.

- If possible, use this time to sleep in a place where your baby won't wake you. Move to a different room, turn on some white noise, and **have confidence in your partner's ability to handle baby's needs**. Finding the right sleep environment when you are not on duty to feed your baby or be the one to get up if you hear them stirring will help you feel (slightly) more rested.
- Work with your partner to extend this little sleep window to get you (both) as many consecutive hours of quality sleep as possible, especially if and when you (and your doctor) feel comfortable weaning baby from some or all-night feedings.

Learn about newborn sleep to help you set expectations for baby sleep patterns and feel empowered with tools to help improve sleep.

- Consider one of **Taking Cara Babies' online sleep classes**.

These **free or inexpensive sleep resources** are great starting points:

- Taking Cara Babies has blog posts with sample (flexible) schedules to help with sleep (takingcarababies.com):

    o *5 Things Every Expectant Mom Needs to Know About Baby Sleep*
    o *Newborns and Naps*

- Mom's On Call (momsoncall.com):

    o *Nap Schedules: 5 to 25 Months*

- Healthychildren.org:

    o *Tips for Getting Your Baby to Sleep*

You are not a failure if your baby isn't sleeping through the night or getting long stretches of sleep. Keep trying, keep learning, and, as long as everyone is safe, keep doing what feels right for your family's situation —maybe a different approach is working or feels better for you!

No matter how you get through it, remember that this phase doesn't last forever—you will sleep again!

DAILY LIFE

Find daily shortcuts!

- Use disposable paper products for some (or all) meals for a few weeks.
- If it fits into your family's budget, splurge on cooking shortcuts.

    o Stock up on frozen meals. Trader Joe's has great options.
    o Say okay to an extra night of food delivery.
    o If you don't have a Keurig, an Instant Pot, or a slow cooker, **add it to the cart**!

- Find little ways to make parenting tasks easier, like choosing swaddles and outfits for sleep and play with zippers or Velcro.

PHYSICAL + MENTAL HEALTH

- Call your doctor or your baby's pediatrician if you are concerned about something. Instead of going down rabbit holes of Google search results and reading horror stories from other moms in the comment section that may increase your anxiety, find out how to contact your family's health provider(s) for questions or concerns about your baby's health or your health postpartum.
- Your healthcare provider can give you direction, advise you if you need to be seen by a doctor, and make a note to discuss a specific concern at your next appointment.
- Agree on a **code word** you can use with your partner to say, "I'm at the end of my rope and need a little help here." For example, if it's your turn in the middle of the night but you can't handle another

second of it this particular time, you can communicate this with your code word. Consider it your family's SOS signal to ask for help without having to explain why.

- **Forgive your partner** quickly during any exhaustion/stress-induced arguments when you first get home. It will get easier just when you think you can't take anymore. Give yourself some grace. Expect some good moments and some difficult ones. Let go when you can. It's okay if you don't set up a one-month-old photo on exactly the right day (or ever). It's okay if you don't fit tummy time in this afternoon. It's okay if the third nap of the day wasn't on schedule or didn't happen at all. No new mom has ever done this perfectly!

Recognize if you are falling into a comparison trap and stop the social media scroll.

- While social media can be a fun way to connect and share your little one with loved ones, acknowledge when you might need to disconnect. There are times when the *running on empty/ first-time-mom-fog* can make you feel too overwhelmed by how Courtney gave birth *four times* and still has great hair or what milestones she checked off on her baby's adorable chalkboard chart. Even though it's great to cheer for all the mamas who showered today, all the littles conquering milestones, and even Courtney and her fantastic hair, it is okay to need a break sometimes. Scroll through your camera roll instead and focus on all that makes your little one their own version of perfect.

- Have options for easy, mindless, uplifting activities to fill the *too-tired- to-be-productive* moments. Listen to a podcast. Escape into a good book or audiobook. Reach out to someone who makes you laugh, even if you haven't responded to other texts all week.

Find little ways to indulge that make you feel like yourself.

- Take 10 minutes to do something that helps you relax. Skip the laundry. Light a candle. Turn on some music. Take a bath. Try a new face mask.
- Try a 10-minute guided meditation or body scan. Just remember to set an alarm if you think you may fall asleep.

Go Outside.

- If you and your baby can safely go outside, fresh air helps in ways you may not even realize. If you can't get outside, open your blinds to let in some natural light. You could even try an artificial light source like a light therapy lamp. As always, consult your doctor or pediatrician about your chosen products and how often to use them.
- In a Journal of Sleep Research study, 6-12 week-old babies who slept well at night were exposed to more light during the day (Harrison, 2004).

Postpartum Depression (PPD) + Anxiety (PPA) Information

One in seven women, or about 15%, develop postpartum depression, and about half have never experienced depression before (March of Dimes, 2019). PPD and PPA are medical conditions without a single cause. They **affect moms across all socioeconomic statuses, ethnicities, education levels, and ages**. Familiarize yourself with possible symptoms now to ensure that you and your support system are well-equipped to recognize them and take swift action to get help.

Possible PPD symptoms include (March of Dimes, 2019):

- often feeling sad, worthless, tired, or disinterested in things you normally like
- having severe mood swings (including frequent crying or rage)
- experiencing significant changes in your eating or sleeping habits
- having a tough time bonding with your baby
- thinking about hurting your baby or yourself

Possible PPA symptoms include (Cleveland Clinic, 2022):

- frequently fearing, worrying about, or obsessing over events unlikely to happen
- having heart palpitations, nausea, loss of appetite, or feeling short of breath
- racing thoughts, often about worst-case scenarios
- being overly cautious about situations that aren't dangerous (e.g., feeling scared to leave your baby alone with your spouse or a trusted adult)

GETTING HELP

If you are concerned that you may be susceptible to or are experiencing depression or anxiety, it is very important to get the help, support, and treatment that is available to you to keep you and your baby safe.

- **Talk to your OB/GYN, your baby's pediatrician, a primary care provider or a mental health provider** anytime, including before giving birth.
- Your provider may recommend counseling (Cognitive Behavioral or Interpersonal Therapy), support groups, and/or medicine as treatment.

ADDITIONAL RESOURCES

- Learn more about postpartum depression at *postpartumdepression.org*.
- Register for an online support meeting led by Postpartum Support International.
- The Substance Abuse and Mental Health Services Administration (SAMHSA) website will help you find mental health treatment facilities and programs in your state.

Postpartum Depression + Anxiety Resources

MY OB/GYN: _____

BABY'S PEDIATRICIAN: _____

NATIONAL SUICIDE PREVENTION HOTLINE AND WEBSITE:

- Call or Text:
  - **988** or **1-800-273-8255** (*English*)
  - **988** or **1-888-628-9454** (*En Español*)
- Chat: 988lifeline.org
- Free and confidential, available 24/7/365

POSTPARTUM SUPPORT INTERNATIONAL HELPLINE:

- **1-800-944-4773 (4PPD)**
- Note that this is not an emergency hotline, but someone from the HelpLine will return your call as soon as possible.

FOR CRISES, CALL 988 IF YOU ARE IN CRISIS, HELP IS AVAILABLE.

NATIONAL CRISIS TEXT LINE:

- Text **HOME** to **741741** from anywhere in the USA, anytime, about any type of crisis.

NATIONAL DOMESTIC VIOLENCE HOTLINE:

- Call: **1-800-799-SAFE (7233)**
- Text: **START** to **88788**
- **Chat:** thehotline.org
- Free and confidential, available 24/7/365

If you find yourself **at your wit's end** and you know that all of your baby's needs have been met (food/diaper/burped/etc.), **put your baby down somewhere you know they will be safe (e.g., bare crib or bassinet)** and walk away for a few minutes to **gather yourself**. If your baby is safe, it is okay if they cry or even wail. Let yourself cry, take a breath, say a prayer, take a shower, call a friend, or do whatever it takes to make yourself feel a little better.

Quick Ways to Calm Down

1 BOX BREATHING

- Inhale for a count of 4.
- Hold your breath gently for a count of 4.
- Exhale for a count of 4.
- Hold your breath gently for a count of 4.
- Repeat 4 times.

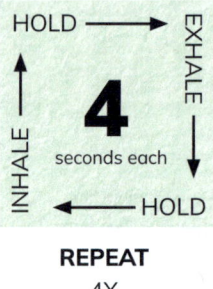

HOLD → EXHALE

4 seconds each

INHALE ← HOLD

REPEAT 4X

REMEMBER:
- If you are prone to hyperventilating or having panic attacks, **check with your doctor** before doing any controlled breath-work.
- If you need to **put baby down** while you gather yourself, make sure to put him or her in a safe place, like a bare crib.

2 REPEAT A MANTRA OR AFFIRMATION

"THIS WILL NOT LAST FOREVER."	*"I am a good parent having a tough time."*
"With every breath, I feel more relaxed."	"I AM SAFE. MY BABY IS SAFE."

"ONE THING AT A TIME."

3 MEDITATE

Try listening to a free **10-minute guided meditation** or body scan on YouTube. Incorporating this into your daily routine may help reduce overall anxiety. Remember to set an alarm before you start if you think you may fall asleep!

4 WRITE DOWN YOUR FEELINGS

Write down your feelings in a journal. Try categorizing them into four emotions: **Glad, Sad, Mad, Scared**. Journaling your feelings may relieve some stress and may help you identify triggers in the future.

Organize + Feel Your Feelings

DATE: _October 27_

Glad

- Enjoyed spending time with Anna at the park celebrating her birthday.
- Michael put away the laundry and did the dishes, so I had quality time to work on my side business after work.
- Grandma Grace got my card wishing her a speedy recovery for her broken wrist.

Mad

- Waited on hold with IRS for 30 minutes before the automated message hung up on me —so aggravating!
- Chris' tone in our meeting felt disrespectful.
- Haven't been sleeping well, and I feel like my fuse is shorter than usual.

Sad

- Saw on social media that Jess was in town, and she didn't reach out to meet up. Feels like a one-way friendship lately.
- Feel guilty that I wasn't paying attention when Michael was telling me a story he was interested in about the NBA game.

Scared/Anxious

- A little nervous for the results of the glucose tolerance test tomorrow...
- Team is asking if I'll return to work after 6 weeks. I don't know if I'll be ready.
- Still need to decide if we're going to Chelsea's wedding in Seattle (baby will only be 3 months old - so many logistics if we decide to go).

Grateful

- The sunset tonight was so beautiful!
- Dad's mechanic fixed the car today for half the cost that the dealership quoted.
- Great Aunt Susan sent us the cutest homemade quilt for baby.

I'm so relieved to be in bed right now. I'm wearing my favorite pajamas, I have a cup of water with 85 ice cubes, and I've already brushed my teeth. I'm going to sleep early because I have to be up early for my glucose test tomorrow.

I should probably look up what I am allowed to eat beforehand...I'm so excited to meet this little baby.

Organize + Feel Your Feelings

DATE: _____

Glad	Mad

Sad	Scared/Anxious

Grateful

_____

_____

_____

Caring for Your New Baby

While you'll likely be in the swing of things pretty quickly once your baby arrives, consider trying these tips, tricks, and shortcuts that may help you along the way.

DIAPER CHANGES + BLOWOUTS

- Instead of trying to take your baby's onesie off from the bottom up, use the onesie's top flaps, which are specifically designed for this purpose, and take it off from the top down. Just fold the flaps down over the shoulders and down the arms and then legs until it is completely off.
- Consider a wipeable changing pad cover for easy cleaning and disinfecting. Another option is an easy-clean changing pad that can be wiped without having to wash a cover.
- Consider a portable changing mat or a travel diaper mat both at home and on the go.
- Keep some laundry detergent and stain remover near a sink where you can wash out stains before they set in/before you're ready to do a full load of laundry.
- If your baby is having a lot of blowouts, it may be time to try the next size up in diapers, even before baby reaches the "recommended" weight for that diaper size. Sizing up and pulling the tabs tight may help.

- After using a wet wipe, dry off the area with a dry cloth to help prevent diaper rash.
- Once your baby starts reaching or rolling, keep some toys near the diapers so you are ready to keep your baby distracted and in place (small bubbles, a teething toy, a ball or rattle, a crinkle book).

BATH TIME

- For bath time in colder months, heat the room by running the shower for a few minutes. Bring what you need to change the baby in the warm bathroom on a changing pad afterward rather than carrying them to a colder room.
- Give baby something (teething toy, toothbrush, bath toy, etc.) to keep little hands busy as baby becomes more interested in grabbing whatever soap or bottle you are using.
- Use something for your knees and (maybe even your elbows) like soft folded towels, a yoga mat, a memory foam bath mat, or a bath kneeler with elbow rest to keep yourself comfortable while leaning over the tub.

Keep baby extra safe in the tub:

- Make sure there isn't a shower head or shampoo/soap on a soap stand that could fall unexpectedly and hit your baby's head.
- Consider an anti-slip mat if your baby is on the go in the tub. Hang it to dry, and follow care instructions to prevent moisture from being trapped in the tub.
- Be mindful of the water spout, or cover it with a washcloth or bath spout cover if baby may bump into it.

SOOTHING A FUSSY BABY

- Try Dr. Harvey Karp's "Five S's for Soothing Babies" (2003):

  ○ Swaddle
  ○ Side-stomach position (for holding baby)
  ○ Shush (make a consistent "shushing sound" that matches the volume of your baby's cry)
  ○ Swing (use a rocking or swaying motion to soothe baby with motion)
  ○ Suck (offer your baby a pacifier or clean finger)
  ○ Watch Dr. Karp demonstrate or read more about this pediatrician's suggested techniques on his website, *Happiestbaby.com.*

- Try gently bouncing on an exercise ball to soothe your baby with motion.
- Try Taking Cara Babies' Top Ten Tips for Witching Hour: Cara demonstrates how to soothe a baby with a swaddle and warm water. She also suggests decreasing stimulation or even getting in the bath together.

- Try taking your baby outside or going for a walk. Fresh air and nature may do wonders for both of you.

Introducing simple sign language signs can help older babies (8 months+) communicate.

Consider introducing the signs for:

  ○ More, All Done
  ○ Eat, Milk
  ○ Help, Please, Thank You
  ○ Potty/Bathroom

- Check out the *"How to start signing with your baby"* video by My Smart Hands.
- Review the Baby Sign Dictionary and watch video demonstrations of baby sign language.

ON-THE-GO

- Stash extra diapers and wipes in your car. Remember to replace them when the baby moves up to the next size.
- Store small diaper bag items in clear pouches so they are easier to grab and find.
- Keep wet/dry bags in your diaper bag in case you need to bring something home to wash later.
- If a car seat strap gets twisted, it is important to untwist it for safety purposes. Move the buckle to the bottom of the strap and **pinch the strap above the buckle in a triangle shape. Slide the buckle up and over the triangle shape,** and the strap will be untwisted.

WAYS TO SAVE

- Once Upon a Child is a nationwide secondhand baby store with nearly everything you could imagine for clothes, gear, and toys. Items are generally well-organized, and you can often find clothes with the tags still on.
- If you plan to create a baby registry, consider registering with promotions such as discounts, welcome boxes, and samples.
- If you plan to formula feed, sign up for coupons.
- Diaper brands often offer loyalty programs where you can earn rewards for using their products.
- Buy diapers and wipes in bulk from membership warehouse clubs like Costco or watch for sales at general merchandise retailers like Target and Walmart.
- Check with your insurance to see if you are eligible for a free breast pump.

FEEDING

It may be helpful to try multiple burping techniques after feeding your baby:

- On your chest or shoulder
- Sitting on your lap
- Face down across your lap

The Taking Cara Babies blog demonstrates different burping techniques and shows how a "normal" amount of spit-up can **look** like a lot. This visual may help you better understand the number of ounces your baby is spitting up per feeding. Of course, talk to your pediatrician about how much your baby is spitting up, especially if you are concerned.

CREATING SLEEP HABITS

Following a (flexible) schedule can help set up good habits during the newborn phase.

- Sleep > eat > age-appropriate wake window > sleep > eat > wake window (repeat)
- Try feeding your baby when they wake up rather than while falling asleep.
- Feeding your baby as soon they wake up can give them energy for their awake time and may help avoid them relying on milk to fall back asleep.
- If you're trying to wake your baby in the middle of a feed, open their onesie or change their diaper.
- For white noise, you can use a household fan, a mobile app, or a white noise machine. Set the white noise to be about **as loud as a shower running**.
- Learning approximately how much sleep babies need at different ages and after how much "awake time" they may be ready for a nap can help.
- Learning about babies' "sleep cues" can help prevent over-tiredness.
- Your baby may prefer a certain pacifier, so it can be helpful to try different kinds.
- Consider swaddling your baby for night sleep and naps to create a womb-like environment (Moon et al., 2022).

  - An easy-to-use swaddle with Velcro or zippers can help make this process easier.
  - After weaning your baby from a swaddle, they can use a sleep sack to stay warm and cozy while sleeping.

- Having your baby sleep in a dark room with white noise and introducing a bedtime or nap-time routine may help cue them that it is time for sleep.

A pre-sleep routine can be simple:

- o Darken the room and turn on the sound machine.
- o Change baby's diaper.
- o Put on baby's swaddle or sleep sack (age depending)
- o Offer a pacifier.
- o Read a book, sing a song, or gently rock your baby.
- o Place your baby in the bassinet or crib.

● If you'd like additional sleep suggestions, a sleep class can help you feel hopeful and empower you with expert-approved tools to help you and your baby get better sleep.

REMEMBER: If your baby isn't sleeping through the night or getting long stretches of sleep, **you are not a failure**. Keep trying, keep learning, and (as long as everyone is safe) keep doing what feels right for your family's situation. Maybe a different approach is working for you or feels better for you! No matter how you get through it, remember this phase doesn't last forever— **you will sleep again**!

Simple Responses to New Mom FAQs

+ UNSOLICITED ADVICE

Becoming a new mom can feel like you're a celebrity (a possibly sweaty and definitely tired one, but still!). Family and friends often go out of their way to shower you with gifts, compliments, and love. We can also expect a lot of love coming via texts, video calls, and phone calls. Sometimes, it can feel overwhelming to keep up with replying to so many different people on different platforms while also trying to take care of a newborn.

Consider using these go-to-responses for your family and friends' frequently asked questions. No one's judging if you copy and paste these to multiple people!

When you're in the trenches as a new mom, anything that makes life a little easier counts for A LOT.

"When can I meet baby?"

*If you're **not planning to allow visitors**:*
- We would absolutely love to see you, but right now, we're playing it super safe until [baby's name] has had more time to build up their immune system. I am counting down the days until we can all be together again! In the meantime, would you be up for a video call?

*If you're **planning to allow visitors** with specific precautions in place:*
- We would absolutely love to see you. Right now, we're playing it super safe until [baby's name] has had more time

to build up their immune system. We're asking people to [add your rules like wearing a mask, washing hands, and keeping some distance] if they come over to meet [baby's name]. Would that be okay with you? If not, we can set up a video call.

REMEMBER: When dealing with a particularly pushy person, you can always default to the pediatrician with a "our pediatrician recommended..." line.

"How are you!? Do you need anything?" (especially during the 4th trimester)

*If you feel like you could use a **break from cooking/dishes**:*
- We're doing [great, well, okay, etc.]! Thanks so much for asking. I've been going non-stop since we got home from the hospital. Honestly, the only thing that would make our lives easier right now would be having a meal delivered.

*If you feel like you could use some **moral support**:*
- We're doing [okay]! Thanks so much for asking. I've been going non-stop since we got home from the hospital. I know I'm supposed to sleep when the baby sleeps, but I could really use a [video call, phone call, etc.] with you! Is there a time that works for you [today, tomorrow, this week]?

*If you feel like you could use **a helping hand**:*
- We're doing [okay]! Thanks so much for asking. I've been going non-stop since we got home from the hospital. Would you be up for coming over sometime this week? I would love to see you and could use an extra pair of hands!

*If you feel like you're **running on empty** and could use a break:*
- We're doing [okay]! Thanks so much for asking. I've been going non-stop since we got home from the hospital. Would you be available to come over to watch [baby's name] for a bit sometime this week? I feel like I'm getting burnt out and could really use a break.

REMEMBER: If you are concerned about perinatal mood and anxiety disorders (anytime during pregnancy or through the first year postpartum), including postpartum depression or anxiety, call your doctor or call the **Postpartum Support International Help Line** at **1-800-944-4773** (4PPD) for help finding local resources, or call **988** if you are in crisis.

"Does baby need anything?"

*If your **baby could use something** or if you know they'd like to get a gift:*
- Thanks so much for asking! Just when I feel like [baby's name] has everything they could dream of, [baby's name] hits a new milestone and needs something else! Right now, they are loving [tummy time, playing with toys, eating solids, reading books, bath-time, etc.], so a [toy, bib, book, etc.] would be amazing!

*If you prefer to **decline the offer**:*
- Thanks so much for asking! [Baby's name] has everything they could dream of! It would be so fun if they could see you on a video call, though. I want [baby's name] to recognize you next time we're together!

"Is baby sleeping through the night yet?"

- We're starting to get into a routine with [baby's name]'s sleep, which is all we can ask for at this point!
- Right now, we're getting a few hour stretches at a time, which is pretty typical for this age, but we're looking forward to that when they're ready!

"Is he/she a good baby?"

This is a silly question, but people ask it often for whatever reason. Providing a generic answer seems to do the trick.
- [Baby's name] is a great baby!
- Yes! I love [baby's name] so much!
- Definitely! We've learned so much already, and we're starting to get into a good routine.

"Are you breastfeeding?"

You'll be surprised by how many people will ask you this. Why do they care? What difference does it make to them? There aren't any good answers to those questions, but some potential responses are:

If you'd rather not answer:
- I don't really feel comfortable discussing that.
- I'd rather not discuss that.
- That's a little too personal.
- Why don't you tell me about your experience with breastfeeding?

If you are and want to respond:
- Yes - so far, so good.
- Yes. We're finally starting to get into a groove now!

If you're not and want to respond (keep in mind you can always just say "No," but sometimes it feels more natural to say a little more):
- Nope. It didn't feel like the right fit for us.
- No, but we've already found a formula they love!

If you're supplementing or transitioning to formula:
- Sometimes—we do a little of both.
- No, but after trying it, I have a new appreciation for the moms who do!
- Not anymore—we transitioned to formula.

What to Say When You're Caught-Off-Guard by Unsolicited Advice

Once your little one makes their appearance, people will say the WILDEST things to you. Men suddenly become experts on breastfeeding and pumping. Non-parents compare raising your human baby to their dog baby. Your mother-in-law will insist you add rice cereal to your week-old baby's bottle. Your neighbor will diagnose your baby as bowlegged and flat-headed. These simple responses can help shut down these (usually) well-intentioned people politely.

I'M GLAD YOU MENTIONED THAT. I'M GOING TO LOOK MORE INTO IT.

THAT'S INTERESTING.
I hadn't thought of it that way before.

I just follow the pediatrician's recommendations.

It sounds like that worked well for you and your child, but it may not be right for us.

I will keep that in mind. Thanks!

I appreciate that you want to help, but I am comfortable with the approach I'm taking and would appreciate if you'd understand that.

IT SOUNDS LIKE SO MUCH HAS CHANGED OVER THE YEARS!

Sample Daily Schedule

WEEKS 1-6

The best way to approach the first few months with a newborn is to **prioritize flexibility and your baby's specific needs**. Sample schedules simply provide you with an idea of what a day with your newborn *might be like*. You will find a rhythm eventually, but the first few weeks can often feel like an endless cycle of feeding, changing diapers, and trying to nap when your baby does. It will get easier!

Time	AM/PM	Activity
6–7	AM/PM	Diaper + Feed + Awake Time
7–9	AM/PM	Nap
9–10	AM/PM	Diaper + Feed + Awake Time
10–12	AM/PM	Nap
12–1:30	AM/PM	Diaper + Feed + Awake Time
1:30–3	AM/PM	Nap
3–4	AM/PM	Diaper + Feed + Awake Time
4–6	AM/PM	Nap
6–7	AM/PM	Diaper + Feed + Bedtime Routine
7–9	AM/PM	Night Sleep
9–9:30	AM/PM	Diaper + Feed
9:30–12	AM/PM	Night Sleep
12–12:30	AM/PM	Diaper + Feed
12:30–3	AM/PM	Night Sleep
3–3:30	AM/PM	Diaper + Feed
3:30–6	AM/PM	Night Sleep

FEEDING BASICS

FREQUENCY + AMOUNT:
Breastfeeding: For infants, it is typically recommended to breastfeed on demand according to your baby's hunger cues. Very young infants often breastfeed about every 2-3 hours (8-12 times) per day for 20-30 minutes per feeding.
Bottles: Infants who are bottle-fed pumped milk or formula typically eat 1-3 ounces per feeding every 2-3 hours.
TYPICAL HUNGER CUES:
- Mouth opening/lips smacking/tongue out
- Moving head side-to-side
- Hands to mouth
- Nuzzling head to breasts
- Fussing
- Crying and turning red

(Jain & AAP, 2022)

SLEEP BASICS

AVERAGE WAKE WINDOW
A wake window is the amount of time a baby is awake between naps. For the first few weeks, your baby will typically only be awake for 30 minutes to an hour at a time before they are ready for their next nap.
AVERAGE LENGTH OF NAP:
30 to 120 minutes
AVERAGE TOTAL DAILY SLEEP:
14-17 hours
TYPICAL SLEEP CUES:
- Staring into the distance or looking away
- Rubbing eyes or yawning
- Crying, arching back, or clenching fists

(Children's Hospital of Philadelphia, n.d.)

DAILY DIAPER COUNT

AVERAGE # PEE DIAPERS: 5-6+
AVERAGE # POO DIAPERS: 0-1
Check with your pediatrician if your baby is not making enough wet (pee) diapers per day or has more than 8 hours between pee diapers. This can be a sign of dehydration; **your doctor will help your baby get back on track**.

(South Dakota Department of Health, 2022)

First Car Seat

1 READ + INSTALL

- Always refer to your **specific car seat manufacturer's guide**.
- Read your **vehicle owner's manual** regarding how to use the seat belt **or** latch method (not both), which seat the car seat can be installed in, if the seat in front of it can touch the car seat, etc.
- According to the National Highway Traffic Safety Administration (2023), **a child under age the age of 1 should always ride in a rear-facing** infant or convertible **car seat**.

MODEL: _____

PURCHASE DATE: _____

EXPIRATION DATE: _____

INFANT INSERT WT LIMIT: _____

HT LIMIT: _____

WT LIMIT: _____

---

2 CHECK

- [ ] Car seat is **not expired**.
- [ ] Car seat is **rear-facing**.
- [ ] A car seat installed properly **should not move more than an inch** side-to-side or front-to-back if you tug where the seat belt or lower anchor strap goes through the seat.
- [ ] If the infant car seat has a handle, check your car seat's guide for the **correct handle position** when in motion.
- [ ] For rear-facing car seats, the shoulder straps should come out of the seat **at or below the shoulders**. Straps must not be twisted.
- [ ] The 5-point harness is secured, with the chest clip at **armpit level**.
- [ ] Tug the straps to **tighten the hidden slack** at baby's hip and torso.
- [ ] Try the **"pinch test"** to ensure the straps are tight enough. Pinch each shoulder strap vertically. If you can grasp any material between your fingers, it's too loose. Tug the harness adjuster to tighten.

- [ ] Baby falls **within weight and height limits** of the car seat (and infant insert, if applicable).

3 REMEMBER

- Do not allow your baby to sleep in the car seat outside the car.
- If your baby is awake in the car seat outside of the car, keep the 5-point harness secured until you are ready to take your baby out completely.
- Do not use aftermarket/3rd party products that did not come with your car seat (e.g., support pillows, shoulder pads, custom covers, etc.).
- During winter, take off baby's coat before strapping them in. Place layer(s) on top of baby after they are securely buckled into the car seat.

Labor
Day

Hospital Bag Checklist

FOR LABOR

- [ ] Folder, pen, notepaper
- [ ] Driver's license
- [ ] Insurance card
- [ ] Hospital forms
- [ ] Birth plan
- [ ] Water bottle

_____

_____

FOR MOM

- [ ] 1-2 hospital gown alternatives
- [ ] Big, comfortable underwear
- [ ] Big T-shirt and shorts/pajama pants
- [ ] Prenatal vitamins
- [ ] Socks (with grips)
- [ ] Nursing bras or big sports bras
- [ ] Lanolin nipple cream

_____

_____

FOR THE PARENT(S)

- [ ] Toiletries
- [ ] Towels/washcloths
- [ ] Shower shoes
- [ ] Pillow and blanket
- [ ] Long charging cable for phones
- [ ] Laptop/iPad
- [ ] Clothes for going home
- [ ] Cash (vending machine, valet, etc.)
- [ ] Snacks
- [ ] Medications

FOR BABY

- [ ] Car seat
- [ ] Diaper bag essentials

_____

_____

OTHER REMINDERS

- [ ] Pet: Food/treats for 3-4 days

_____

_____

_____

_____

ADDITIONAL NOTES

_____

_____

_____

_____

Essential Documents

FOR THE HOSPITAL

- [ ] **YOU + PARTNER'S ID (E.G., DRIVER'S LICENSE)**
- [ ] **HEALTH INSURANCE CARD**
- [ ] **PEDIATRICIAN CONTACT INFORMATION**
- [ ] **BIRTH PREFERENCES/PLAN**
- [ ] **HOSPITAL ADMISSIONS PAPERWORK**
- [ ] **SOCIAL SECURITY CARD (OR MEMORIZE YOUR SSN)**
- [ ] **LIST OF MEDICATIONS**
- [ ] **MARRIAGE CERTIFICATE (IF APPLICABLE)**
- [ ] **CORD BLOOD PAPERWORK (IF APPLICABLE)**

ADDITIONAL NOTES

Diaper Bag Essentials

- ☐ OUTFITS (PREEMIE, NB, OR 0-3M)
- ☐ HAT
- ☐ SOCKS + MITTENS
- ☐ BURP CLOTHS
- ☐ COMB/HAIRBRUSH
- ☐ LOTION
- ☐ PACIFIER
- ☐ SWADDLE OR SWADDLE BLANKET
- ☐ PEDIATRICIAN CONTACT INFO

ADDITIONAL NOTES

LABOR DAY

Pediatrician Contact Information

Pediatrician Name: _____

Office Name: _____

Phone Number: _____ **Fax Number:** _____

Email: _____

Office Address: _____

_____

_____

When to call to schedule first appointment: _____

_____

_____

_____

ADDITIONAL NOTES

_____

_____

_____

_____

_____

_____

_____

_____

_____

_____

_____

_____

Baby's Birth Statistics

Date: _____   Time: _____ : _____ AM / PM

Weight at Birth: _____ LB _____ OZ   Weight at Discharge: _____ LB _____ OZ

Length: _____ IN/CM   Apgar Score: 1 MIN: _____ 5MIN: _____

Head Circumference: _____ IN/CM   Blood Type: _____

NEWBORN SCREENING RESULTS

HEARING	PASS / NONPASSING
PULSE OXIMETRY	PASS / NONPASSING
BLOOD SPOT	IN RANGE / BORDERLINE / OUT OF RANGE

ADDITIONAL NOTES

_____

_____

_____

_____

_____

_____

_____

_____

_____

_____

Questions to Ask the Doctor After Delivery

BEFORE LEAVING THE HOSPITAL

BABY

How often should I feed the baby? _____

_____

_____

If breastfeeding, how long should I breastfeed for (per breast)? _____

_____

_____

_____

If formula feeding, how much formula should I be feeding? _____

_____

_____

_____

How often should the baby be peeing? Pooping? _____

_____

_____

_____

What color should the pee and poop be? _____

_____

_____

How long should we track feedings and diapers? _____

_____

_____

Can we use a pacifier? _____

_____

_____

How do we take care of the umbilical cord? What should I do if it starts bleeding? What are the signs of infection?

_____

_____

_____

When should we give the first bath? How often? Sponge bath or submerged?

_____

_____

_____

If circumcised, how do we properly care for it? What are the signs of infection?

_____

_____

When should we check the baby's temperature? What temperature is too high/too low? Which method should we use?

_____

_____

GENERAL

What amount of pain and bleeding should I expect, and for how long? What are possible causes for concern?

_____

_____

Are there any symptoms I should call you about or return to the hospital for?

_____

_____

Can you confirm the baby's records are being sent to the pediatrician?

_____

_____

Where can I obtain the cost of treatment? _____

_____

_____

If planning to formula feed, how do I dry up my milk? _____

_____

_____

When should I schedule my next appointment at the OBGYN?

_____

_____

Where can I find resources if I am struggling with PPD/PPA?

_____

_____

Should I continue taking my prenatal vitamins? How long?

_____

_____

_____

When can I be intimate again? _____

_____

_____

When can we introduce the baby to family and friends? What precautions should we take when doing so?

_____

_____

_____

What temperature should we keep our home? Do we need to use a humidifier?

_____

_____

VAGINAL RECOVERY

Should I use a stool softener? If so, for how long?

_____

_____

How long should I use the bathroom items such as the peri bottle, sitz bath, etc.?

_____

_____

Should I do pelvic floor exercises? If so, which ones?

_____

_____

If applicable, do the stitches dissolve on their own?

_____

_____

How long will I bleed? What kind of blood clots are normal?

_____

_____

C-SECTION RECOVERY

How do I best care for my incision? _____

_____

_____

What do you recommend for pain management? _____

_____

_____

What do you recommend for scar care? _____

_____

_____

When and how will any stitches be removed? _____

_____

_____

Can I use an abdominal binder? _____

What activities can I/can't I do? _____

_____

_____

When can I drive? _____

How much weight am I allowed to lift/carry? (Baby, car seat, etc.?)

_____

How long will I be swollen for? _____

Will I experience numbness? _____

What are signs of infection to look out for? _____

_____

Food, Diaper + Sleep Log

DATE: __January 17__

Write today's date.

TIME	NURSE MINS	PUMP OZ / ML	BOTTLE OZ / ML	DIAPER	SLEEP
(AM) PM 6:30	(LEFT) RIGHT 15 15	LEFT RIGHT		🟡 ✓🟤	START / END 7:38 8:30
(AM) PM 8:45	LEFT (RIGHT) 12	LEFT RIGHT 3 2.5	2.5	✓🟡 ✓🟤	START / END 9:50 10:22
AM 10:30		RIGHT		✓🟡 🟤	START / END 12:07 1:52
AM		RIGHT			START / END
AM		RIGHT			START / END
AM PM	LEFT RIGHT	LEFT RIGHT			START / END
AM PM	LEFT RIGHT	LEFT RIGHT		🟡 🟤	START / END
AM PM	LEFT RIGHT	LEFT RIGHT		🟡 🟤	START / END
AM PM	LEFT RIGHT	LEFT RIGHT		🟡 🟤	START / END
AM PM	LEFT RIGHT	LEFT RIGHT		🟡 🟤	START / END

Circle whichever side you start on for that session.

Mark if the diaper was pee (yellow) or poo (brown) or leave blank if neither.

Food, Diaper + Sleep Log

DATE: _____ / _____ / _____

TIME	NURSE MINS		PUMP OZ / ML		BOTTLE OZ / ML	DIAPER		SLEEP
AM PM	LEFT	RIGHT	LEFT	RIGHT		●	●	START / END
AM PM	LEFT	RIGHT	LEFT	RIGHT		●	●	START / END
AM PM	LEFT	RIGHT	LEFT	RIGHT		●	●	START / END
AM PM	LEFT	RIGHT	LEFT	RIGHT		●	●	START / END
AM PM	LEFT	RIGHT	LEFT	RIGHT		●	●	START / END
AM PM	LEFT	RIGHT	LEFT	RIGHT		●	●	START / END
AM PM	LEFT	RIGHT	LEFT	RIGHT		●	●	START / END
AM PM	LEFT	RIGHT	LEFT	RIGHT		●	●	START / END
AM PM	LEFT	RIGHT	LEFT	RIGHT		●	●	START / END
AM PM	LEFT	RIGHT	LEFT	RIGHT		●	●	START / END

Food, Diaper + Sleep Log

DATE: _____ / _____ / _____

TIME	NURSE MINS	PUMP OZ / ML	BOTTLE OZ / ML	DIAPER	SLEEP
AM PM	LEFT RIGHT	LEFT RIGHT		● ●	START / END
AM PM	LEFT RIGHT	LEFT RIGHT		● ●	START / END
AM PM	LEFT RIGHT	LEFT RIGHT		● ●	START / END
AM PM	LEFT RIGHT	LEFT RIGHT		● ●	START / END
AM PM	LEFT RIGHT	LEFT RIGHT		● ●	START / END
AM PM	LEFT RIGHT	LEFT RIGHT		● ●	START / END
AM PM	LEFT RIGHT	LEFT RIGHT		● ●	START / END
AM PM	LEFT RIGHT	LEFT RIGHT		● ●	START / END
AM PM	LEFT RIGHT	LEFT RIGHT		● ●	START / END
AM PM	LEFT RIGHT	LEFT RIGHT		● ●	START / END

Food, Diaper + Sleep Log

DATE: _____ / _____ / _____

TIME	NURSE MINS		PUMP OZ / ML		BOTTLE OZ / ML	DIAPER	SLEEP
AM PM	LEFT	RIGHT	LEFT	RIGHT		● ●	START / END
AM PM	LEFT	RIGHT	LEFT	RIGHT		● ●	START / END
AM PM	LEFT	RIGHT	LEFT	RIGHT		● ●	START / END
AM PM	LEFT	RIGHT	LEFT	RIGHT		● ●	START / END
AM PM	LEFT	RIGHT	LEFT	RIGHT		● ●	START / END
AM PM	LEFT	RIGHT	LEFT	RIGHT		● ●	START / END
AM PM	LEFT	RIGHT	LEFT	RIGHT		● ●	START / END
AM PM	LEFT	RIGHT	LEFT	RIGHT		● ●	START / END
AM PM	LEFT	RIGHT	LEFT	RIGHT		● ●	START / END
AM PM	LEFT	RIGHT	LEFT	RIGHT		● ●	START / END

Food, Diaper + Sleep Log

DATE: _____ / _____ / _____

TIME	NURSE MINS		PUMP OZ / ML		BOTTLE OZ / ML	DIAPER	SLEEP
AM PM	LEFT	RIGHT	LEFT	RIGHT		● ●	START / END
AM PM	LEFT	RIGHT	LEFT	RIGHT		● ●	START / END
AM PM	LEFT	RIGHT	LEFT	RIGHT		● ●	START / END
AM PM	LEFT	RIGHT	LEFT	RIGHT		● ●	START / END
AM PM	LEFT	RIGHT	LEFT	RIGHT		● ●	START / END
AM PM	LEFT	RIGHT	LEFT	RIGHT		● ●	START / END
AM PM	LEFT	RIGHT	LEFT	RIGHT		● ●	START / END
AM PM	LEFT	RIGHT	LEFT	RIGHT		● ●	START / END
AM PM	LEFT	RIGHT	LEFT	RIGHT		● ●	START / END
AM PM	LEFT	RIGHT	LEFT	RIGHT		● ●	START / END

Food, Diaper + Sleep Log

DATE: _____ / _____ / _____

TIME	NURSE MINS		PUMP OZ / ML		BOTTLE OZ / ML	DIAPER		SLEEP
AM PM	LEFT	RIGHT	LEFT	RIGHT		●	●	START / END
AM PM	LEFT	RIGHT	LEFT	RIGHT		●	●	START / END
AM PM	LEFT	RIGHT	LEFT	RIGHT		●	●	START / END
AM PM	LEFT	RIGHT	LEFT	RIGHT		●	●	START / END
AM PM	LEFT	RIGHT	LEFT	RIGHT		●	●	START / END
AM PM	LEFT	RIGHT	LEFT	RIGHT		●	●	START / END
AM PM	LEFT	RIGHT	LEFT	RIGHT		●	●	START / END
AM PM	LEFT	RIGHT	LEFT	RIGHT		●	●	START / END
AM PM	LEFT	RIGHT	LEFT	RIGHT		●	●	START / END
AM PM	LEFT	RIGHT	LEFT	RIGHT		●	●	START / END

Additional Resources

Baby's Important Information

FOR PARENTS

Name: _____

DOB: _____ / _____ / _____   **SNN:** _____   **Blood Type:** _____

Allergies: _____

Medications: _____

Health Conditions: _____

Hospital: _____

Childcare Contact Name: _____

Childcare Contact Phone #: _____

US Poison Control #: (800) 222-1222   **US National Battery Ingestion #: (800) 498-8666**

Doctor's Name + #	Insurance Company + Policy #
Pediatrician	
Dentist	
Optometrist	

LOCATION OF IMPORTANT PAPERWORK

Birth Certificate: _____

Social Security Card: _____

Parent's Will: _____

College/Savings Account(s): _____

Other: _____

Other: _____

Emergency Information

TO LEAVE WITH A CAREGIVER

FOR EMERGENCIES, CALL 911

PARENT(S)

Name: _____   Phone #: _____

Name: _____   Phone #: _____

EMERGENCY

Hospital Name: _____   Hospital Address: _____

Emergency Contact: _____   Phone #: _____

US Poison Control #: (800) 222-1222   US National Battery Ingestion #: (800) 498-8666

CHILD

Name: _____

Age: _____   DOB: _____ / _____ / _____   Blood Type: _____

Allergies: _____

Medication: _____

Health Conditions: _____

DOCTOR

Name: _____

Phone #: _____

Address: _____

DENTIST

Name: _____

Phone #: _____

Address: _____

INSURANCE

Name: _____

Group #: _____

ID #: _____

HOUSE INFORMATION

Home Address: _____

First Aid Kit: _____   Fire Extinguisher: _____

Water Shut-Off Valve: _____   Gas Shut-Off Valve: _____

Electrical Panel: _____   Flashlights: _____

Front Door Code: _____   Garage Code: _____

WiFi Network: _____   WiFi Password: _____

Additional Info: _____

Baby's Daily Schedule

TO LEAVE WITH A CAREGIVER

AM
PM
_____

AM
PM
_____

AM
PM
_____

AM
PM
_____

AM
PM
_____

AM
PM
_____

AM
PM
_____

AM
PM
_____

AM
PM
_____

AM
PM
_____

AM
PM
_____

AM
PM
_____

AM
PM
_____

AM
PM
_____

AM
PM
_____

AM
PM
_____

AM
PM
_____

AM
PM
_____

Name: _____ **DOB:** _____

Pediatrician Name: _____

Pediatrician #: _____

Insurance Co: _____

Insurance Policy #: _____

Poison Control: _____

ADDITIONAL NOTES:

_____

_____

_____

_____

REMINDERS:

_____

_____

_____

_____

ADDITIONAL RESOURCES

156

Baby's Daily Schedule

TO LEAVE WITH A CAREGIVER

_____
AM
PM
_____
AM
PM
_____
AM
PM
_____
AM
PM
_____
AM
PM
_____
AM
PM
_____
AM
PM
_____
AM
PM
_____
AM
PM
_____
AM
PM
_____
AM
PM
_____
AM
PM
_____
AM
PM
_____
AM
PM
_____
AM
PM
_____
AM
PM
_____
AM
PM
_____
AM
PM

Name: _____ DOB: _____

Pediatrician Name: _____

Pediatrician #: _____

Insurance Co: _____

Insurance Policy #: _____

Poison Control: _____

ADDITIONAL NOTES:

_____

_____

_____

_____

REMINDERS:

_____

_____

_____

_____

Medication Tracker

Medication: _____   **Dosage:** _____

Reason: _____   **Start Date:** _____

Notes: _____

_____

_____

DATE	AM	AM	PM	PM	NOTES

Medication Tracker

Medication: _____ **Dosage:** _____

Reason: _____ **Start Date:** _____

Notes: _____

_____

_____

DATE	AM	AM	PM	PM	NOTES

Medical Treatment Authorization

Minor's Name: _____

Home Address: _____

Date of Birth: _____ / _____ / _____   Sex: _____

MEDICAL INFORMATION

Primary Care Physician's Name: _____

Primary Care Physician Phone Number: _____

Medical Insurance Provider: _____ Policy #: _____

Preferred Hospital/Treatment Center: _____

Allergies to Medications: _____

Medical conditions for which the minor currently receives treatment: _____

_____

Prescription drugs the minor is taking: _____

_____

Additional medical information: _____

_____

AUTHORIZATION AND CONSENT OF PARENT(S) OR LEGAL GUARDIAN(S)

As custodian of the aforementioned minor, I give my authorization and consent for _____ to provide general first-aid treatment for minor illnesses and/or injuries. If the illness and/or injury is severe, I permit them to find professional emergency personnel to attend, transport, and treat the minor. I permit them to issue consent for medical care recommended by a licensed medical professional or institution. I also permit the designated adult to exercise the best judgment based on the advice of medical or emergency personnel.

Mother/Guardian's Name: _____

Phone: _____ Email Address: _____

Father/Guardian's Name: _____

Phone: _____ Email Address: _____

Parent/Guardian Signature: _____ Date: _____

Printed Name: _____

Parent/Guardian Signature: _____ Date: _____

Printed Name: _____

Medical Treatment Authorization

Minor's Name: _____

Home Address: _____

Date of Birth: _____ / _____ / _____   **Sex:** _____

MEDICAL INFORMATION

Primary Care Physician's Name: _____

Primary Care Physician Phone Number: _____

Medical Insurance Provider: _____   **Policy #:** _____

Preferred Hospital/Treatment Center: _____

Allergies to Medications: _____

Medical conditions for which the minor currently receives treatment: _____

_____

Prescription drugs the minor is taking: _____

_____

Additional medical information: _____

_____

AUTHORIZATION AND CONSENT OF PARENT(S) OR LEGAL GUARDIAN(S)

As custodian of the aforementioned minor, I give my authorization and consent for _____
to provide general first-aid treatment for minor illnesses and/or injuries. If the illness and/or injury is severe, I permit them to find professional emergency personnel to attend, transport, and treat the minor. I permit them to issue consent for medical care recommended by a licensed medical professional or institution. I also permit the designated adult to exercise the best judgment based on the advice of medical or emergency personnel.

Mother/Guardian's Name: _____

Phone: _____   **Email Address:** _____

Father/Guardian's Name: _____

Phone: _____   **Email Address:** _____

Parent/Guardian Signature: _____   **Date:** _____

Printed Name: _____

Parent/Guardian Signature: _____   **Date:** _____

Printed Name: _____

FOR EMERGENCIES, CALL 911

Food, Diaper + Sleep Log

DATE: _____ / _____ / _____

TIME	NURSE MINS	PUMP OZ / ML	BOTTLE OZ / ML	DIAPER	SLEEP
AM PM	LEFT RIGHT	LEFT RIGHT		● ●	START / END
AM PM	LEFT RIGHT	LEFT RIGHT		● ●	START / END
AM PM	LEFT RIGHT	LEFT RIGHT		● ●	START / END
AM PM	LEFT RIGHT	LEFT RIGHT		● ●	START / END
AM PM	LEFT RIGHT	LEFT RIGHT		● ●	START / END
AM PM	LEFT RIGHT	LEFT RIGHT		● ●	START / END
AM PM	LEFT RIGHT	LEFT RIGHT		● ●	START / END
AM PM	LEFT RIGHT	LEFT RIGHT		● ●	START / END
AM PM	LEFT RIGHT	LEFT RIGHT		● ●	START / END
AM PM	LEFT RIGHT	LEFT RIGHT		● ●	START / END

Food, Diaper + Sleep Log

DATE: _____ / _____ / _____

TIME	NURSE MINS	PUMP OZ / ML	BOTTLE OZ / ML	DIAPER	SLEEP
AM PM	LEFT RIGHT	LEFT RIGHT		● ●	START / END
AM PM	LEFT RIGHT	LEFT RIGHT		● ●	START / END
AM PM	LEFT RIGHT	LEFT RIGHT		● ●	START / END
AM PM	LEFT RIGHT	LEFT RIGHT		● ●	START / END
AM PM	LEFT RIGHT	LEFT RIGHT		● ●	START / END
AM PM	LEFT RIGHT	LEFT RIGHT		● ●	START / END
AM PM	LEFT RIGHT	LEFT RIGHT		● ●	START / END
AM PM	LEFT RIGHT	LEFT RIGHT		● ●	START / END
AM PM	LEFT RIGHT	LEFT RIGHT		● ●	START / END
AM PM	LEFT RIGHT	LEFT RIGHT		● ●	START / END

Food, Diaper + Sleep Log

DATE: _____ / _____ / _____

TIME	NURSE MINS	PUMP OZ / ML	BOTTLE OZ / ML	DIAPER	SLEEP
AM PM	LEFT RIGHT	LEFT RIGHT		● ●	START / END
AM PM	LEFT RIGHT	LEFT RIGHT		● ●	START / END
AM PM	LEFT RIGHT	LEFT RIGHT		● ●	START / END
AM PM	LEFT RIGHT	LEFT RIGHT		● ●	START / END
AM PM	LEFT RIGHT	LEFT RIGHT		● ●	START / END
AM PM	LEFT RIGHT	LEFT RIGHT		● ●	START / END
AM PM	LEFT RIGHT	LEFT RIGHT		● ●	START / END
AM PM	LEFT RIGHT	LEFT RIGHT		● ●	START / END
AM PM	LEFT RIGHT	LEFT RIGHT		● ●	START / END
AM PM	LEFT RIGHT	LEFT RIGHT		● ●	START / END

Food, Diaper + Sleep Log

DATE: _____ / _____ / _____

TIME	NURSE MINS	PUMP OZ / ML	BOTTLE OZ / ML	DIAPER	SLEEP
AM PM	LEFT RIGHT	LEFT RIGHT		🟡 🟤	START / END
AM PM	LEFT RIGHT	LEFT RIGHT		🟡 🟤	START / END
AM PM	LEFT RIGHT	LEFT RIGHT		🟡 🟤	START / END
AM PM	LEFT RIGHT	LEFT RIGHT		🟡 🟤	START / END
AM PM	LEFT RIGHT	LEFT RIGHT		🟡 🟤	START / END
AM PM	LEFT RIGHT	LEFT RIGHT		🟡 🟤	START / END
AM PM	LEFT RIGHT	LEFT RIGHT		🟡 🟤	START / END
AM PM	LEFT RIGHT	LEFT RIGHT		🟡 🟤	START / END
AM PM	LEFT RIGHT	LEFT RIGHT		🟡 🟤	START / END
AM PM	LEFT RIGHT	LEFT RIGHT		🟡 🟤	START / END

Food, Diaper + Sleep Log

DATE: _____ / _____ / _____

TIME	NURSE MINS	PUMP OZ / ML	BOTTLE OZ / ML	DIAPER	SLEEP
AM PM	LEFT RIGHT	LEFT RIGHT		⬤ ⬤	START / END
AM PM	LEFT RIGHT	LEFT RIGHT		⬤ ⬤	START / END
AM PM	LEFT RIGHT	LEFT RIGHT		⬤ ⬤	START / END
AM PM	LEFT RIGHT	LEFT RIGHT		⬤ ⬤	START / END
AM PM	LEFT RIGHT	LEFT RIGHT		⬤ ⬤	START / END
AM PM	LEFT RIGHT	LEFT RIGHT		⬤ ⬤	START / END
AM PM	LEFT RIGHT	LEFT RIGHT		⬤ ⬤	START / END
AM PM	LEFT RIGHT	LEFT RIGHT		⬤ ⬤	START / END
AM PM	LEFT RIGHT	LEFT RIGHT		⬤ ⬤	START / END
AM PM	LEFT RIGHT	LEFT RIGHT		⬤ ⬤	START / END

Food, Diaper + Sleep Log

DATE: _____ / _____ / _____

TIME	NURSE MINS	PUMP OZ / ML	BOTTLE OZ / ML	DIAPER	SLEEP
AM PM	LEFT RIGHT	LEFT RIGHT		⬤ ⬤	START / END
AM PM	LEFT RIGHT	LEFT RIGHT		⬤ ⬤	START / END
AM PM	LEFT RIGHT	LEFT RIGHT		⬤ ⬤	START / END
AM PM	LEFT RIGHT	LEFT RIGHT		⬤ ⬤	START / END
AM PM	LEFT RIGHT	LEFT RIGHT		⬤ ⬤	START / END
AM PM	LEFT RIGHT	LEFT RIGHT		⬤ ⬤	START / END
AM PM	LEFT RIGHT	LEFT RIGHT		⬤ ⬤	START / END
AM PM	LEFT RIGHT	LEFT RIGHT		⬤ ⬤	START / END
AM PM	LEFT RIGHT	LEFT RIGHT		⬤ ⬤	START / END
AM PM	LEFT RIGHT	LEFT RIGHT		⬤ ⬤	START / END

Food, Diaper + Sleep Log

DATE: _____ / _____ / _____

TIME	NURSE MINS	PUMP OZ / ML	BOTTLE OZ / ML	DIAPER	SLEEP
AM PM	LEFT RIGHT	LEFT RIGHT		● ●	START / END
AM PM	LEFT RIGHT	LEFT RIGHT		● ●	START / END
AM PM	LEFT RIGHT	LEFT RIGHT		● ●	START / END
AM PM	LEFT RIGHT	LEFT RIGHT		● ●	START / END
AM PM	LEFT RIGHT	LEFT RIGHT		● ●	START / END
AM PM	LEFT RIGHT	LEFT RIGHT		● ●	START / END
AM PM	LEFT RIGHT	LEFT RIGHT		● ●	START / END
AM PM	LEFT RIGHT	LEFT RIGHT		● ●	START / END
AM PM	LEFT RIGHT	LEFT RIGHT		● ●	START / END
AM PM	LEFT RIGHT	LEFT RIGHT		● ●	START / END

Food, Diaper + Sleep Log

DATE: _____ / _____ / _____

TIME	NURSE MINS	PUMP OZ / ML	BOTTLE OZ / ML	DIAPER	SLEEP
AM PM	LEFT RIGHT	LEFT RIGHT		● ●	START / END
AM PM	LEFT RIGHT	LEFT RIGHT		● ●	START / END
AM PM	LEFT RIGHT	LEFT RIGHT		● ●	START / END
AM PM	LEFT RIGHT	LEFT RIGHT		● ●	START / END
AM PM	LEFT RIGHT	LEFT RIGHT		● ●	START / END
AM PM	LEFT RIGHT	LEFT RIGHT		● ●	START / END
AM PM	LEFT RIGHT	LEFT RIGHT		● ●	START / END
AM PM	LEFT RIGHT	LEFT RIGHT		● ●	START / END
AM PM	LEFT RIGHT	LEFT RIGHT		● ●	START / END
AM PM	LEFT RIGHT	LEFT RIGHT		● ●	START / END

Organize + Feel Your Feelings

DATE: _____ / _____ / _____

Glad	Mad

Sad	Scared/Anxious

Grateful

_____

_____

_____

Organize + Feel Your Feelings

DATE: _____ / _____ / _____

Glad	Mad

Sad	Scared/Anxious

Grateful

_____

_____

_____

Organize + Feel Your Feelings

DATE: _____ / _____ / _____

Glad	**Mad**
Sad	**Scared/Anxious**

Grateful

_____

_____

_____

Organize + Feel Your Feelings

DATE: _____ / _____ / _____

Glad	Mad

Sad	Scared/Anxious

Grateful

_____

_____

_____

Organize + Feel Your Feelings

DATE: _____/_____/_____

Glad	Mad

Sad	Scared/Anxious

Grateful

_____

_____

_____

Organize + Feel Your Feelings

DATE: _____ / _____ / _____

Glad	Mad

Sad	Scared/Anxious

Grateful

_____

_____

_____

Notes

References

American Academy of Pediatrics [AAP]. (2022a, June 21). *American Academy of Pediatrics Updates Safe Sleep Recommendations: Back is Best* [Press release]. https://www.aap.org/en/news-room/news-releases/aap/2022/american-academy-of-pediatrics-updates-safe-sleep-recommendations-back-is-best/

American Academy of Pediatrics [AAP]. (2022b, August 15). *Baby Walkers: A Dangerous Choice.* HealthyChildren.org. https://www.healthychildren.org/English/safety-prevention/at-home/Pages/Baby-Walkers-A-Dangerous-Choice.aspx

American Academy of Pediatrics [AAP]. (2023, May 1). *Car Seats: Information for Families.* HealthyChildren.org. https://www.healthychildren.org/English/safety-prevention/on-the-go/Pages/Car-Safety-Seats-Information-for-Families.aspx

American Pregnancy Association. (n.d.-a). *First-Trimester Screening.* https://americanpregnancy.org/prenatal-testing/first-trimester-screening/

American Pregnancy Association. (n.d.-b). *Prenatal Tests.* https://americanpregnancy.org/prenatal-testing/prenatal-tests/

American Pregnancy Association. (2021). *Counting Baby Kicks.* American Pregnancy Association. https://americanpregnancy.org/healthy-pregnancy/while-pregnant/counting-baby-kicks

Bhaskar, S. (2021, March 16). *Mold in Bath Toys.* ChildrensMD. https://childrensmd.org/browse-by-topic/safety/mold-in-bath-toys/

Centers for Disease Control and Prevention [CDC]. (2022a, January 24). *Proper Storage and Preparation of Breast Milk.* Centers for Disease Control and Prevention. https://www.cdc.gov/breastfeeding/recommendations/handling_breastmilk.htm

Centers for Disease Control and Prevention [CDC]. (2022b, March 18). *Pregnancy.* Centers for Disease Control and Prevention. https://www.cdc.gov/oralhealth/fast-facts/pregnancy

Centers for Disease Control and Prevention [CDC]. (2023a, May 16). *Infant Formula Preparation and Storage.* Centers for Disease Control and Prevention. https://www.cdc.gov/nutrition/infantandtoddlernutrition/formula-feeding/infant-formula-preparation-and-storage.html

Centers for Disease Control and Prevention [CDC]. (2023b, June 9). *Parasites - Toxoplasmosis (Toxoplasma infection).* Centers for Disease Control and Prevention. https://www.cdc.gov/parasites/toxoplasmosis

Children's Hospital of Philadelphia. (n.d.). *Newborn-Sleep Patterns.* https://www.chop.edu/conditions-diseases/newborn-sleep-patterns

Children's Rehabilitation Institute TeletonUSA. (2020, April 30). *Caution with walkers, jumpers, exersaucers.* Children's Rehabilitation Institute TeletonUSA (CRIT). https://critusa.org/caution-with-walkers-jumpers-exersaucers/

Cleveland Clinic. (2022, April 12). *Postpartum Anxiety.* https://my.clevelandclinic.org/health/diseases/22693-postpartum-anxiety

DiMaggio, D. & American Academy of Pediatrics [AAP]. (2023, January 23). *Inclined Sleepers, Crib Bumpers & Other Baby Registry Items to Avoid.* HealthyChildren.org. https://www.healthychildren.org/English/ages-stages/baby/sleep/Pages/Inclined-Sleepers-and-Other-Baby-Registry-Items-to-Avoid.aspx

Harrison, Y. (2004), *The relationship between daytime exposure to light and night-time sleep in 6–12-week-old infants.* Journal of Sleep Research, 13: 345-352. https://doi.org/10.1111/j.1365-2869.2004.00435.x

Illinois Department of Public Health [IDPH]. (2021, May 10). *NIPT Information for Obstetric Care Providers.* Illinois Department of Public Health. https://dph.illinois.gov/topics-services/life-stages-populations/genomics/fact-sheets/nipt-providers.html

International Hip Dysplasia Institute. (2020, December 15). *Hip-Healthy Swaddling - International Hip Dysplasia Institute.* International Hip Dysplasia Institute -. https://hipdysplasia.org/infant-child/hip-healthy-swaddling/

Jain, S. & American Academy of Pediatrics [AAP]. (2022, May 13). *How Often and How Much Should Your Baby Eat?* HealthyChildren.org. https://www.healthychildren. org/English/ages-stages/baby/feeding-nutrition/Pages/ how-often-and-how-much-should-your-baby-eat.aspx

Karp, H. (2003). *The happiest baby on the block: The New Way to Calm Crying and Help Your Newborn Baby Sleep Longer.* Bantam.

LaBotz, M. (2020, May 22). *Out of the Container, and Onto the Floor.* American Academy of Pediatrics. https:// publications.aap.org/journal-blogs/blog/4236/Out-of- the-Container-and-Onto-the-Floor

March of Dimes. (2019, March). *Postpartum depression.* https://www.marchofdimes.org/find-support/topics/ postpartum/postpartum-depression

March of Dimes. (2020, April). *Caffeine in pregnancy.* https://www.marchofdimes.org/find-support/topics/ pregnancy/caffeine-pregnancy

March of Dimes. (2022, March 29). *Doulas can improve care before, during, and after childbirth.* https://www. marchofdimes.org/find-support/blog/doulas-can- improve-care-during-and-after-childbirth

Moon, R. & American Academy of Pediatrics [AAP]. (2022, July 14). *How to Keep Your Sleeping Baby Safe: AAP Policy Explained.* HealthyChildren.org. https://www. healthychildren.org/English/ages-stages/baby/sleep/ Pages/a-parents-guide-to-safe-sleep.aspx

Moon, R., Glassy, D., & American Academy of Pediatrics [AAP]. (2022, July 15). *Swaddling: Is it Safe for Your Baby?* HealthyChildren.org. https://www.healthychildren. org/English/ages-stages/baby/diapers-clothing/Pages/ Swaddling-Is-it-Safe.aspx

National Domestic Violence Hotline. (n.d.-a). *Domestic Violence Support.* https://www.thehotline.org/

National Domestic Violence Hotline. (n.d.-b). *How to Stay Physically, Emotionally and Financially Safe During Pregnancy.* The Hotline. https://www.thehotline.org/ resources/staying-physically-emotionally-and- financially-safe-during-pregnancy/

National Highway Traffic Safety Administration [NHTSA]. (2023, June 14). *Car Seats and Booster Seats.* National Highway Traffic Safety Administration. https:// www.nhtsa.gov/equipment/car-seats-and-booster-seats

Nguyen, T. P. & Nemours Children's Health. (2022, July). *Prenatal Tests: First Trimester.* Nemours KidsHealth. https://kidshealth.org/en/parents/tests-first-trimester. html

Safe Sleep for Babies Act of 2021, H.R.3182, 117th Cong. (2021). https://www.congress.gov/bill/117th- congress/house-bill/3182

South Dakota Department of Health. (2022, September 21). *Feeding Guide: 0-5 Months. South Dakota WIC.* https://sdwic.org/wic_library/children/feeding-guides/ feeding-guide-0-5-months/

U.S. Department of Agriculture [USDA]. (2020, May 11). *Safe Minimum Internal Temperature Chart.* U.S. Department of Agriculture Food Safety And Inspection Service. https://www.fsis.usda.gov/food-safety/safe- food-handling-and-preparation/food-safety-basics/ safe-temperature-chart

U.S. Department of Health & Human Services. (2020, September 25). *People at Risk: Pregnant Women.* FoodSafety.gov. https://www.foodsafety.gov/people-at- risk/pregnant-women

U.S. Department of Labor. (n.d.). *Family and Medical Leave Act.* https://www.dol.gov/agencies/whd/fmla

U.S. Food and Drug Administration [FDA]. (2022, January). *Food Safety Booklet for Pregnant Women, Their Unborn Babies, and Children Under Five | FDA.* U.S. Food And Drug Administration. https://www.fda.gov/ media/83740/download

Wiessinger, D., West, D., J Smith, L., & Pitman, T. (2018, November 28). *The Safe Sleep Seven.* La Leche League International. https://llli.org/the-safe-sleep-seven/

Acknowledgments

First off, thank you, pregnant mom-to-be. Thank you to all the moms who came before me and made it look so easy that I thought having a baby would be as easy as having a puppy (hint: there's no overnight doggie daycare equivalent for babies). To my late grandmothers, to whom I wish I could ask about their pregnancies, birth stories, and how they managed so many babies without grocery delivery and dishwashers. To my multi-billion dollar employer that doesn't offer paid maternity leave, thank you for lighting a fire in me to advocate for new moms, with the first step in the form of this book. Thank you, best mom-friends Brinya + Ashley, who have offered solidarity during the challenges and humor during the absurdity.

Thank you, Mom and Dad, for supporting me every step of the way and for loving our boys. Thank you, Nanny, for being my loudest cheerleader! Thank you, **Carter Kenai**, for making me a first-time mom, and **Mack Jay**, for making me a second-timer. Thank you, **Brandon Jerrell**, for our two boys and for always encouraging me to find my why.

Michelle Newman

Thank you to the women bearing the highs and lows of motherhood for lightening the load just by sharing in this knowing. Thank you to my own village for showing up for me and my little loves, especially when I could not. Thank you, Mom, for loving us, and now, our babies with so much joy and grit. Thank you, Sis, Mom 2, for making my journey our journey. Thank you, Michelle, for giving me a lifeline and a laugh every time I need one and for being brave enough to share that lifeline with any mom who reads this book.

And thank you **Mark, Larkin, Elin**, and **Casen**, for this wild and beautiful life.

Brinya Van Guilder

Author Biographies

Michelle Newman was so ready to be a mom. How hard could it be? Fast forward to March 2020, when her son Carter was born just outside New York City. Eight days in as a first-time mom: cue global shutdown, stay-at-home orders, social isolation, and shattered hopes and dreams for a "normal" (unpaid) maternity leave. Global pandemic aside, why had she felt like she read and researched every possible piece of information while pregnant, only to find out she was NOT actually prepared to take care of the baby? Michelle vowed that her pregnant friends would not be as confused/overwhelmed/surprised as she was. What started as text messages and a spreadsheet transformed into a blog and then a book. Michelle is a fierce advocate for new moms and hopes that sharing the information she has learned will be valuable to other new moms navigating the (sometimes choppy) waters!

Brinya Guilder is a new mom to three, simultaneously drowning and delighting in the daily debacles the title brings. Brinya has slowly learned to laugh at how unprepared she was when her son Larkin was born in 2019, despite her many well researched to-do lists. When Brinya's friend Michelle joined her as a new mom, they recognized a shared passion for collecting shortcuts and showing solidarity through the messy moments of mothering. Brinya's twins (surprise!) were born in 2023, and she is as determined as ever to help new moms and to laugh with them along the way.

Thank you!

Thank you for reading our book!

We would really appreciate your feedback
and would love to hear what you
have to say. We need your input to make
the next version of this book and
our future books better.

Please take two minutes now to leave a
helpful review on Amazon, letting us know
what you thought of the book:

www.stresslessmom.com/reviews

Thank you so much!

Michelle Newman and Brinya Van Guilder

Made in United States
Troutdale, OR
01/04/2025

27500430R00106